THE LITTLE BOOK OF LONDON

DAVID LONG

WITH ILLUSTRATIONS BY LES EVANS

THE HISTORY PRESS

First published in the United Kingdom in 2007 by
Sutton Publishing, an imprint of NPI Media Group Limited
Cirencester Road · Chalford · Stroud · Gloucestershire · GL6 8PE

Reprinted in 2008 by The History Press

British Library Cataloguing in Publication Data
A catalogue record for this book is available from the British
Library.

ISBN 978-0-7509-4800-5

For my mother, Ellen Long, with love and gratitude

Typeset in 9/12.5pt Sabon.
Typesetting and origination by
The History Press.
Printed and bound in England.

CONTENTS

———◆◈◆———

INTRODUCTION

I t's a city most Londoners think they know pretty well, and one with which most visitors quickly feel familiar. Yet the truth is that some of the most fascinating, frivolous and bizarre facts about London – all the really important stuff, in other words – are the ones most people simply never get to hear about. Stuff they don't even realise they don't know. Stuff like this:

Arriving in London from Oxford in 1662, Christopher Merrett demonstrated how to make champagne at a meeting of the Royal Society, doing so a full thirty years before Dom Perignon managed to do it in France.

When 1960s guitar legend Jimi Hendrix moved into Brook Street and found he was living next door to Handel's Mayfair mansion he went straight out and bought himself a recording of the *Messiah*.

Never mind that dodgy kebab, the most unappetising meal ever served in London was almost certainly the inaugural dinner of the Society for the Acclimatisation of Animals in the United Kingdom in 1862. The menu included rhino pie and porpoise heads, panther cutlets, kangaroo steak and stew, and Japanese sea-slug soup.

The earliest known reference to mud-wrestling in London was in the 1730s when bouts were regularly held in the pleasure gardens at Belsize Park. Eventually the revels got so out of hand the place had to be closed down in 1745.

The world's first ever traffic island was installed in 1864 so its inventor Colonel Pierpoint could cross the street to reach his club. Unfortunately when he turned to admire his creation the Colonel tripped over and was knocked down by a cab.

By 1900 there were nearly 300,000 horses employed in the capital. Eating up to a million tons of food a year between them, each one deposited three to four tons of dung on the capital's crowded streets.

Lost property handed in to London Transport personnel over the years has included a lawnmower, several silicon breast implants, a bishop's crook and a puffer fish, an outboard motor from a boat, an entire garden bench, a sealed box containing three dead bats, an artificial leg, several glass eyes, one stuffed gorilla, two human skulls in a bag, a wheelchair and a wedding dress. Each year approximately 7,000 mobile phones are left behind on tube trains and buses, together with an average of two bikes a week.

In 1868 London's first ever traffic light blew up killing a policeman and causing a passing platoon of cavalry to stampede.

With a range of 30 miles, the main guns of HMS *Belfast* are targeted on Barnet and if fired would destroy Scratchwood Services on the M1.

CRIME & PUNISHMENT

BEHEADINGS, BURNINGS & HANGINGS

When Charles II's illegitimate son, the Duke of Monmouth, was executed for treason in 1685 it took executioner Jack Ketch five blows of the axe and the job still had to be finished off with a knife. The two halves were apparently then promptly recovered in order that his severed head could be sewn back on and the corpse made to sit for a royal portrait.

In the days when hangings at Tyburn were routine, the gallows (which stood on a spot near the south-west corner of modern Connaught Square) could accommodate twenty-one men or women at a time. Convention dictated the order of precedence so that highwaymen as the 'aristocrats of crime' were despatched first, then common thieves, with traitors being left to bring up the rear.

During the long procession from Newgate Gaol in the City to the so-called 'Tyburn Tree', the condemned were presented with scented nosegays by crowds which could number up to 10,000. Convicts could also enjoy a last drink at a tavern, The Mason's Arms, which is still standing in Seymour Place.

French watchmaker Robert Hubert was hanged at Tyburn after confessing to responsibility for the Great Fire in 1666. Needless to say it was a stitch-up, but in fact the death penalty was routine for setting fire to even a single building at this time, never mind 13,200, and remained so until 1861. (Quite a thought today when an estimated 25 per cent of all London fires are started deliberately.)

By 1688 fewer than fifty offences carried the death penalty but under the Hanoverian kings the number was increased to around 300. Largely implemented to reduce the cost of incarcerating offenders, typical among the new capital crimes were the theft of 5s, causing damage to Westminster Bridge and even impersonating a Chelsea Pensioner.

Restored to its original, pristine elegance and repositioned close to St Paul's, Temple Bar originally provided a convenient place to display the bloody, decapitated heads of traitors. Those of the Rye House Plotters in 1683, for example, were boiled in brine and cumin seed to prevent them being pecked at by birds, after which bystanders could pay a ha'penny to hire a telescope to enjoy a really close look at the gory remains.

London's own 'death row' moved to Pentonville Prison in 1902 when the dreaded Newgate finally closed. Between then and 6 July 1965 when the practice was finally abolished, Crippen, Christie and 118 others were executed here and are still buried beneath the prison garden. The last condemned cell is now a staff room for the probation service.

In days gone by hanging was considered quite humane. Until 1753 women found guilty of murdering their husbands could expect to be burned at the stake instead, although kindly attempts were sometimes made to strangle them before the flames took hold. As late as 1789 Catherine Murphy was despatched in this way, though in her case it was for 'coining', i.e. counterfeiting or clipping the coin of the realm.

It was not unknown for some felons to escape the drop altogether. John 'Half-hanged' Smith earned this soubriquet in 1705 by taking so long to die that the crowd demanded he be cut down and let loose. Patrick O'Bryan was similarly reprieved but on being set free made the mistake of going back to murder his accuser. Back in the dock he was boiled in pitch to ensure the same thing wouldn't happen again.

In 1531 a man called Rouse was boiled alive at Smithfield, a fitting end for a chef. Cook to the Bishop of Rochester, he had been found guilty of accidentally murdering several colleagues while attempting to poison his employer. Boiling for poisoners, however, was removed from the statute books seventeen years later.

Under the 1752 Murder Act the Company of Surgeons and St Bartholomew's and St Thomas's hospitals were each entitled to ten hanged corpses a year for the purposes of dissection and anatomising. Punch-ups frequently broke out when their representatives attempted to claim the bodies, however, because for many dissection was considered to be an ignominy too far.

The largest crowd ever assembled in London for a public execution was that which gathered outside Newgate on 30 November 1824 to see a sentence of hanging carried out on Henry Fauntleroy. An estimated 100,000 people thronged the streets to see the banker die after being convicted of attempting to defraud the Bank of England of £250,000. Money he squandered, which seemed somehow to make the offence even worse.

The last criminals to be publicly beheaded were the five Cato Street conspirators in 1820, although they were decapitated only after they had already been hanged. Similarly the last person to be publicly hanged in London was an Irish nationalist, Michael Barrett, despatched outside Newgate Gaol on 26 May 1868.

The last two executioners employed by the Home Office were Mancunian Harry B. Allen and Robert L. Stewart from Edinburgh. A scaffold is reputed still to exist at Wandsworth, however, making some with an interest in such things wonder whether someone, somewhere, is still being trained up for the job.

In the days when suicide was still illegal, the 'punishment' was to be buried at a crossroads with a stake through one's heart. The last person to suffer such a fate in London was suspected murderer John Williams in December 1811. His corpse, suitably mutilated, lies beneath the tarmac at the junction of New Road and Cannon Street Road, E1.

TOP 10 TORTURES AT THE TOWER

In its day the rack at the Tower of London was known as the Duke of Exeter's Daughter after the nobleman who was appointed Constable of the Tower for life in 1420. After experiencing it, the Catholic martyr Edmund Campion was asked how he felt and replied, 'not ill, because not at all'.

Despite the fact that English Common Law had long ago declared torture to be illegal, the rack was particularly popular under the Tudors. Indeed, during the reign of Elizabeth I, the one in the Tower was said 'seldom to stand idle'.

A later refinement was the sixteenth-century Scavenger's Daughter, a corruption of the name of its inventor Sir Leonard Skevington. This used a pair of iron hoops to crush the body until blood spurted from the nostrils and other orifices. (Even, it was said, from the fingertips).

The use of iron gauntlets required the authority of the Crown or Privy Council, these being devices attached to the wrists and slowly tightened with a screw. The prisoner was then suspended until his arms swelled around the gauntlets. 'I felt', said Father Gerard after trying it out in 1597, 'that all the blood in my body had run into my arms . . . and burst out of my finger ends.' In five hours he claimed to have fainted eight times.

The Tower dungeon known as Little Ease was simplicity itself: a tiny cell of such small dimensions that anyone confined therein could neither stand up, lie down or walk around. Instead those unfortunate enough to be incarcerated were forced to squat painfully in the dark for days on end.

Worse still was the aptly named Dungeon Amongst the Rats. Located below the high-water mark, this dark cell would flood twice a day with malodorous river water. To fall asleep was thus to invite certain death; and even awake a prisoner could find himself surrounded by drowning rats liable in their panic to gnaw at his flesh.

Incredibly *peine forte et dure* or being pressed to death by the weight of stones was not considered to be torture. Thought instead to be more humane than death by starvation, it remained on the statute books until late into the reign of George III. Its 'popularity' derived from the fact that anyone dying this way could will their estates to their descendants instead of being found guilty and made to forfeit everything to the Crown.

Used on those individuals accused of misconduct with Catherine Howard, the brakes was a ferocious device employed to smash the teeth. Fortunately the precise workings of several similar devices – such as the langirnis, the pynebankis and the cashie-laws – can these days only be guessed at.

COURT IN THE ACT

Today's Central Criminal Court, the Old Bailey, stands on the site of the infamous Newgate Gaol. The origin of the name lies in the adjacent street and has been in use since at least the sixteenth century. It is not true, however, that the symbolic figure of Justice with her sword and scales wears a blindfold. The work of sculptor Frederick Pomeroy, RA, she is actually all-seeing.

Despite the name the sixteenth-century 'bawdy courts' were held in St Paul's Cathedral. They dealt with cases of marital or sexual assault and, perhaps out of respect for their surroundings, court clerks adopted a particular euphemism for sexual intercourse which was recorded in all official documents as 'occupying'.

Britain's ancient and much-vaunted jury system is not always what it seems. In 1468, for example, twelve jurors who returned a verdict the judge didn't like were forced to wear dunces' caps, and 200 years later juries were still routinely being locked up without food or water while they reached their decision. What's more, if the judge felt that at the end of it they had reached the wrong one, they would be sent back until they had changed their minds.

Indeed at this same time one jury so upset the judge in a trial of two Quakers that he fined all twelve of them before confining them in Newgate. They were only released on the say-so of a rival judge.

Early judicial proceedings were also astonishingly quick compared to today's. In 1769 in just four days, for example, Old Bailey judges tried no fewer than forty prisoners. Three were executed, twenty-two sentenced to transportation, five 'burnt in the hand' or branded, and a further ten ordered to be whipped.

Even after the Reformation canny criminals could escape punishment by claiming 'benefit of clergy' – i.e. pretending to be in Holy Orders – but they could do this only once. The usual proof required was the ability to read (or more probably recite) one verse of a psalm, since at this time few but the clergy could actually read. Surprisingly, as it was open to such abuse, the practice was still recognised as late as 1847, although for an ever-dwindling range of offences.

The last nobleman to be tried by 'God and his peers' was Lord Edward Southwell Russell de Clifford (1907–66) who in 1935 appeared in the House of Lords on a charge of manslaughter on the Kingston Bypass. The right of peers to be tried by their peers was subsequently abolished by the Criminal Justice Act (1948).

Judges appearing at the Old Bailey today still at certain times carry nosegays of aromatic herbs. This is a tradition harking back to a time when typhus or 'jail fever' was endemic in the Justice Hall of Newgate which stood on the same site. There is of course no evidence that a nosegay provided any protection whatsoever.

CRUEL & UNUSUAL PUNISHMENTS

Preferring mutilation to hanging, branding became popular after the Norman Conquest. Offenders were typically burnt with V marks if they were vagabonds, a T for thieves and an F for a fray – or troublemaking.

Less serious offences generally attracted lesser penalties, although even the pillory was not always the gentle rotten-tomato-flinging affair one might imagine.

Sometimes, for example, the condemned person had his or her ears nailed to the wooden frame for the duration of their ordeal, many being forced to leave one or both of these behind at the end of it.

Others, such as John Waller at Seven Dials in 1732, actually died at the hands of the mob, as did four fraudsters condemned to stand at Newgate in 1756 and hit by a variety of rock-solid objects.

Until the pillory was abolished in 1837, dead cats were a particularly popular missile to hurl at the accused, but even these could be surprisingly dangerous. Anne Morrow, for example, was pilloried at Charing Cross for marrying three times while disguised as a man and was permanently blinded by the objects thrown at her head.

Public whipping was a similarly ferocious affair, offenders sometimes being tied to a tree or whipping post but more often forced to walk a certain route – for example, the length of Fleet Street to Temple Bar – attended by a constable charged with whipping sufficiently hard 'to make the back bloody'.

Flogging for women was finally outlawed in 1820, but the cat-o'-nine-tails remained in use for men until well into the twentieth century. The courts couldn't call for it after 1948, but prison Boards of Visitors were still permitted to and inflicted it on ten prisoners as late as 1954.

Bollards can still be seen next door to Tate Britain, in the courtyard of Chelsea College of Art & Design which occupies the site of the former Millbank Penitentiary. These were once used to tie up the barges used to house prisoners before they were transported to Australia. Indeed the phrase 'down-under' is said to be derived from a tunnel hereabouts, through which they were walked in chains down to the river.

From 1760 to 1774 around 70 per cent of felons convicted at the Old Bailey were transported to the Colonies. Most went to Jamaica and the New World, until American settlers expressed a preference for black slaves over British misfits. Thereafter Australia proved the destination of choice.

Among the first to go to Australia was nine-year-old John Hudson, a chimneysweep who got seven years for stealing some clothes. The same consignment included 82-year-old perjurer Dorothy Handland who killed herself on arrival in Botany Bay, thereby becoming Australia's first known suicide.

Convicted pickpocket Isaac Solomons, widely held to be the prototype for Dickens's Fagin, escaped on his way to Newgate in 1827. He fled the country and sought sanctuary in Tasmania, his wife having already been transported there for crimes of her own. Bizarrely he was then re-arrested, shipped home to London, re-tried, re-convicted, and sentenced to be transported for fourteen years – to Tasmania.

London courts finally stopped sending prisoners to the Colonies in 1868, the last batch arriving in Fremantle, Western Australia.

IN DUNGEONS DIRE

Surprisingly the Tower of London was still functioning as an occasional prison until well into the 1950s. As a result the list of prisoners held there includes not just the likes of Sir Walter Ralegh and Anne Boleyn but also the Nazi Rudolf Hess and even a Kray or two on a charge of desertion.

Perhaps the best accommodated, however, was John II of France. In 1356, when a king's ransom was set at 3,000,000 ecus and took many years to raise, he arrived at the Tower with such a large retinue that the gaolers were even required to house his jester who had come along to cheer him up.

By contrast to King John's luxurious accommodation, the first prisoners sent to Wormwood Scrubs when it opened in 1874 actually had to build their own cells. At least these were arranged in order to catch the sun, but only because the prison's creator Sir Edmund du Cane hoped in this way to solve the lighting and ventilation problems associated with more traditional London gaols.

The largest prison in Britain today, the Scrubs' most famous escapee is probably the Soviet double-agent George Blake who went over the wall in 1966. At the time of his flight to Russia he was just five years into a 42-year sentence, the longest ever handed down by a British court.

Another of the Scrubs' celebrity prisoners was the matinée idol Ivor Novello. In 1944 the actor and composer was arrested and charged with an offence against the wartime petrol-rationing regulations after using a false permit for his Rolls-Royce. Fined £100, he served one month of an eight-week sentence, emerging a broken man and almost certainly forfeiting a knighthood.

The term 'clink' is derived from the Clink Prison in Southwark, originally a private lock-up owned by the bishops of Winchester, and used to house both Protestant and Catholic prisoners of conscience. Destroyed along with several other gaols in the 1780 anti-Catholic Gordon Riots, it was never rebuilt but the name lives on.

Historically London's largest prison, the Millbank Penitentiary was designed to hold 1,500 convicts. The first to be owned and run by the state, it was nevertheless an expensive failure and closed in 1890 less than seventy years after its completion.

Brixton Prison, originally a Surrey House of Correction built in what at the time was described as one of 'the most open and salubrious spots', was sold off by the Home Office in 1851. It had to be bought back two years later, however, when the government decided to imprison women at home rather than transporting them to the Colonies. In 1902 it reverted to a men's prison, as indeed it still is today.

As well as hard labour the prisoners at Brixton were for years required to do not just their own laundry but also the washing sent in by prisoners at Pentonville, Millbank and Wandsworth.

Wandsworth's most famous inmate was Oscar Wilde, who spent six months there in 1895, and second was 'Great Train Robber' Ronnie Biggs who later escaped and fled via Australia to Brazil. Its most pathetic was perhaps William Towens, a child sentenced to serve a month in 1872 after stealing two pet rabbits.

Prison overcrowding is a major problem these days, but it's hardly a new one: Newgate in the City, built to hold 472 prisoners, sometimes accommodated nearly three times this number, hence the interest in using old ships moored on the Thames to hold greater numbers.

Incredibly these 'hulks' were still in use on the Thames until 1857, this despite epidemics of cholera, typhus and scurvy, and obvious problems with rats. They even included two former men o' war from Nelson's fleet at Trafalgar: *Bellerophon* and *Leviathan*. The last to go was the *Defense*, which was finally abandoned and burned at Woolwich Docks.

After the horrors of the hulks (and the many other rat-infested prisons which operated for private profit) Pentonville Prison was state-run and designed along rational or 'model' lines. Established in 1842 and now London's oldest such institution, it was designed as a place where prisoners were to be rehabilitated rather than simply locked up and forgotten. The model for it was a successful correctional facility in Philadelphia.

Even so, with convicts shut in their cells for 23 hours a day, forbidden to talk even to the warders, and forced to wear hoods to prevent them seeing fellow inmates during the one-hour exercise period, mental illness in Pentonville rocketed by more than 1,000 per cent. Fortunately Europe's largest asylum was on the other side of the street, for twenty-two prisoners from the first intake were soon declared insane, twenty-six were found to be suffering from serious delusions, and six hanged themselves in their cells.

Pentonville's advanced theories notwithstanding, gratuitous cruelty continued to be the rule rather than the exception until well into the late nineteenth century. Nevertheless Dickens described the place as too soft, while Thomas Carlyle considered it 'a palace'. This despite a regime which included flogging with the cat, regular confinement on a diet of bread and water, and pointless heavy labour using treadmills and the crank which required felons to push a paddle through sand for hours on end.

CURIOUS FACTS ABOUT COPPERS

Tracing its origins to 1798 and a group of privateers hired by dockland merchants wishing to minimise theft on the water, the Thames River Police is actually the world's oldest surviving police force. (See Chapter 11: The Thames & its Tributaries)

Inspectors in the early days of the Metropolitan Police were permitted to carry pistols but constables were allowed only truncheons. With a band of copper at one end and the Royal monogram WR at the other (for William IV), these quickly gave rise to two enduring nicknames: Coppers and the Old Bill.

Instead of being given vehicles of their own the original batch of Flying Squad officers were at first issued with green and white 'paint-bombs' which could be hurled at any misbehaving motorists as they disappeared down the road.

The Special Branch was formed in 1883, its full name being the Special Irish Branch as it was created expressly in order to deal with the growing menace of Fenian terrorism.

Distinctive blue lamps were installed outside police stations in 1861 in order to identify them to the public. The one at Bow Street, however, was left white in order not to offend the sensibilities of Queen Victoria when she was visiting the opera opposite. (It was thought too tactless a reminder that Prince Albert had died in the Blue Room at Windsor Castle.)

A strange anomaly also meant that Bow Street was funded by the Secret Service rather than the Home Office, and that until 1842 the office remained the personal possession of the Chief Magistrate.

The first bent coppers on record were three senior detectives arrested in 1877 and given two years at the Old Bailey after being found guilty of taking backhanders from conman Harry Benson. (See Chapter 4: Men, Women & Children.)

In theory at least any policeman chasing fugitives into Ely Place, EC1, is required to seek permission before entering the street. As it was the London home of the Bishops of Ely and a private road it was considered technically to be a part of Cambridgeshire. Unusually for London it is still a private thoroughfare.

A high-tech alternative to the traditional truncheon, the Met's 150,000-volt Taser M26 stun gun was first used on a mad Welsh dog, then shortly afterwards (in August 2003) an armed man in Isleworth became its first human target.

LONDON'S LOONIEST LAWS

Members of Parliament enjoy numerous legal privileges when the Commons is in session, but they are still forbidden to attend the House wearing a full suit of armour under the terms of an edict passed by Edward II in 1313.

In Royal Parks it is actually still illegal for people in bathchairs to travel three abreast. Nor – as a result of a byelaw enacted as recently as 1977 – are members of the public permitted to touch a pelican 'except where written permission has been obtained'.

Golfers on Wimbledon Common are allowed to tee off wearing armour if they so wish. In fact they can wear whatever they like providing it includes a pillarbox-red outer garment, a requirement dating back to 1865 when Earl Spencer first gave leave to officers of the London Scottish Rifles to lay out a golf course on what was then his land.

A sign at the foot of the Albert Bridge still requests that approaching soldiers break step to preserve the bridge, although the bridge was actually strengthened in 1884 and then again in the early 1970s.

Freemen of the City of London are still entitled to drive sheep across London's bridges, something last tested by a 60-year-old from Muswell Hill who walked two sheep, Clover and Little Man, across Tower Bridge in 1999. The police stopped him, but after investigating the matter had to let him continue.

Despite the popular cockney singalong ballad, the Metropolitan Police Act of 1839 means Londoners are actually forbidden (on pain of a £20 fine) to roll a barrel down the pavement. More bizarrely still, no-one is allowed to possess a pack of cards 'who lives within a mile of any arsenal or explosives store'.

In Piccadilly's Burlington Arcade one of two top-hatted beadles or watchmen is always on hand to prevent shoppers misbehaving. Specifically shoppers are not allowed to run or to 'walk hurriedly, behave boisterously, sing or whistle'. Opening an umbrella is also an offence, although the rules were recently relaxed to enable them to carry their own shopping.

Her Majesty didn't insist on exercising her prerogative in 2006 when a young whale, apparently lost and confused, made its way up the Thames before dying. However, the reigning monarch has since the Middle Ages been entitled to a share in any such animal The original statute allowed for the head to be presented to the king and for the tail to go to his queen, presumably to provide whalebone for her corsets.

Fortunately Her Majesty has also chosen not to exact the maximum penalty for anyone in the souvenir trade who uses her coat of arms without her permission. A law passed in 1592 calls for such miscreants to be beheaded, and for some reason the crime of 'copying royal emblems' was exempted from the legislation to abolish capital punishment.

Butchers in the City are theoretically still liable to spend a day in a pillory if they knowingly sell bad meat. This 600-year-old law also calls for them to suffer the further indignity of having the offending wares burnt beneath their noses.

Until 1859 it was illegal not to celebrate the arrest of Guido Fawkes on 5 November, and even now children still need the written permission of their local Chief Constable before they can legally knock on doors asking for a penny for the guy.

A charge of 'insulting the king's bard' still carries a substantial fine of six cows and eight pence, although no-one is quite sure these days who, precisely, is the king's bard.

DON'T CALL ME A CAB

Although the horse-drawn Hackney carriage is long gone, London's taxis are technically still governed by a battery of weird rules and regulations, some of which date back to the reign of Queen Anne.

Drivers are still required to carry sufficient foodstuffs for the horse, for example, so that the classic London black cab is still designed with space for a bale of hay next to the driver, and of course with adequate headroom in the back to accommodate a man sporting a top hat.

Some of these laws affect passengers too. You probably didn't know, for example, that if you shout 'Taxi' at a moving vehicle you're breaking the law. What you're supposed to do is go to a taxi rank or what the rules define as 'a place appointed'.

Taxi drivers are also forbidden to carry any passengers suffering from what the law calls a notifiable disease – bubonic plague, that is, or smallpox – and can refuse to pick up anyone they suspect of carrying a contagious disease.

More bizarre still is the regulation (made on the sensible grounds that no driver is allowed to leave his or her cab on the public thoroughfare) requiring the driver to answer the call of nature 'against the rear of the vehicle, and in a seemly fashion'. To this end cabbies are at least permitted to ask a passing police constable to shield them with his (or her) cape.

Finally, while there are laws preventing us from speeding, cabbies who drive too slowly can be charged with 'loitering' or 'driving too furiously' if they are caught speeding within the City boundary.

2

ROYAL LONDON

FIRST AMONG ROYALS

Queen Elizabeth was the first monarch to have her own loo. A portable contrivance invented by her godson Sir John Harington, the invention failed to catch on commercially as Sir John made only two of them and decided to keep the second one for himself.

Henry III was the first English king to die of old age rather than as a consequence of violent intervention or something equally unpleasant.

George V was the first monarch ever to go down a coalmine, and the first to travel to the Middle East since Richard the Lionheart more than 700 years earlier.

Edward VII was the first English monarch to buy a car. He acquired a gigantic 3-litre Renault 14/20 Landaulette after being taken for his first ride in a steam-powered Serpollet by its owner, the chocolate manufacturer Gaston Menier.

Henry IV was the first English king to have English parents.

Henry II was the first king to read a book in bed, George IV the first to wear a kilt in public, and Richard II the first to use a handkerchief – a useful device which he is said to have invented.

Edward VIII was the first bachelor to come to the throne for more than 850 years – the last one had been the Conqueror's son, William Rufus, who was probably homosexual – and the first king ever to have published an autobiography.

George VI was the first sovereign ever to attend a grand prix race – run at Silverstone, in 1950 – but Princess Anne was the first royal to qualify for a Heavy Goods Vehicle licence, and also the one-millionth member of the AA.

Prince Charles is the first heir to the throne to have gone to school, the first to have ridden a killer whale, and perhaps even more surprisingly the first in 300 years to have married an English girl.

Queen Victoria was the first royal to submit to an anaesthetic, agreeing to take chloroform in 1853 at the birth of her son Prince Leopold.

CARRY-ON CORONATIONS

At his coronation Henry IV lost a shoe, then a spur from the other one and finally the wind blew the crown clean off his head.

George III's coronation went on for so long – six hours – that half the congregation sat down to eat, drowning out the ceremony with the clattering of their cutlery.

Prize fighters were engaged to serve as pages at the coronation of George IV, a wise move as his estranged and enraged wife spent much of the day battering at the doors in an attempt to force her way into Westminster Abbey, and wailing loudly when she was unable to do so.

Marking the Restoration of the monarchy, Charles II's coronation had to be postponed once it was discovered that Cromwell had disposed of all the appropriate regalia.

Catholic Mary I refused to sit in the Coronation Chair because she felt it had been defiled by the 'Protestant heretic', her brother Edward VI. As for Queen Anne, she was unable to do so anyway as she was so fat and gout-ridden she had to be carried into the Abbey in a chair of her own.

The Coronation Ring had to be made smaller to fit Queen Victoria, but was then jammed on to the wrong finger by the Archbishop of Canterbury and as a result got stuck.

After the coronation of Edward VII Sir Edward Nichol dismantled His Majesty's robing room at the Abbey and took the panelling home to build a 'motor house' for his two Rolls-Royces.

At George VI's big day an attack of nerves prevented the Lord Chamberlain fixing the Sword of State – His Majesty had to do it himself – then a chaplain fainted, and finally the Archbishop of Canterbury put the crown on back to front.

Clearing up after the Queen's coronation in 1953, cleaners in the Abbey found three ropes of pearls, twenty brooches, six bracelets, twenty golden balls from peers' coronets, most of a diamond necklace, numerous sandwich wrappers and an undisclosed but impressive quantity of half-bottles of spirits (empty).

ENDURING ROYAL SECRETS

It's known that Queen Victoria proposed to Prince Albert, but neither the Queen nor Prince Philip has ever confirmed which one of them took the initiative.

Similarly it has never been publicly revealed what inscription the Duke of Edinburgh had engraved on the royal wedding ring.

Nor has anyone officially confirmed or denied the existence of a secret railway tunnel network linking Buckingham Palace to Heathrow Airport to facilitate a quick escape should republicanism get a grip and the need arise.

Prince Philip has been known to lift the Queen's flagging spirits by reminding her about 'the wailing and gnashing of teeth', although the meaning behind what must be some kind of private joke has yet to be revealed.

STRANGE BUT TRUE

The oldest king ever to ascend the English throne, William IV at the same moment also became William III of Scotland, William II of Ireland and William I of Hanover. He was 64 years and 10 months old.

Travelling in Scotland the Prince of Wales is more correctly known as the Duke of Rothesay.

When it came time to behead Anne Boleyn Henry VIII brought a swordsman over from France to make sure the job was done properly. The Frenchman was paid £23 for his expertise.

One of the Queen Mother's middle names was Angela.

Edward VI had a genuine whipping boy called Barnaby Fitzpatrick who was beaten if the king got his lessons wrong.

Prince Philip is an Admiral of the Fleet in the Royal Australian Navy, the Royal New Zealand Navy and the Royal Canadian Sea Cadets.

Charles I presented his gaoler with a solid gold toothpick on the day of his execution, presumably in the hope of a quick and efficient despatch.

Edward IV was only three years old when he first presided over the official opening of Parliament.

Catherine of Aragon married both Henry VIII and his late brother Arthur. When she died Henry bought himself a bright yellow outfit to celebrate.

George III's mother kept the last official court dwarf in England.

Prince Charles, author of the architectural essay 'A Vision of Britain', also once wrote a 'Guide to the Chatting Up of Girls' but this was never published.

As well as being married to each other the Queen and Prince Philip are second, third and fourth cousins.

When the Queen Mother was a girl she had two pet pigs, named Satan and Emma.

America's infamous Watergate Tapes include a recording of a ninety-minute conversation between Richard Nixon and Prince Charles.

Henry I invented the yard, said to be the measured distance from his nose to his thumb. He had no fewer than twenty-four children, most of whom were illegitimate.

Anne Hyde married James II in private, but nevertheless produced two daughters both of whom became queen (Anne and Mary II).

THE ROYALS AT HOME

As she grew older, and no great mystery here, Good Queen Bess insisted all the mirrors were removed from any rooms she was likely to use.

During the First World War George V famously banned alcohol in the royal households, but kept a regular bottle of port back for himself.

To save money Queen Victoria in 1892 took the decision to replace the royal loo paper with newspaper.

William IV on hearing he was now king went straight back to bed saying 'I've never slept with a queen before'.

The pats of butter served at breakfast at Buckingham Palace have the royal cipher stamped on them.

The Queen's blotting paper is destroyed at the end of every day in order to ensure the confidentiality of anything she may have written.

Prince Philip used to be a smoker but gave it up the day before he married the Queen.

Effectively exiled to France after cutting the staff's beer allowance at Buckingham Palace, the Duke of Windsor took advantage of his diplomatic status to buy all his own drink from duty-free outlets.

Despite John Lennon's insistence that he didn't 'believe in royalty' – perhaps made in retaliation for the Duke of Edinburgh's comment in 1965 that the Beatles were 'on the wane' – *Yellow Submarine* is reportedly one of the Queen's favourite films and one which she has seen many times.

George V's more than 320 stamp albums (now owned by the Queen) are believed to comprise the most valuable such collection in the world.

Edward VII had three washbasins installed in a row at Buckingham Palace, one each for hands, face and brushing his teeth.

Finding lice on his dinner plate in 1787, George III sensibly insisted the kitchen staff all have their heads shaved.

Queen Victoria used to wear an apron around the house and was known to enjoy doodling her royal cipher 'VRI' in the dust on the furniture at Buckingham Palace and Windsor.

The future Edward VIII used to pronounce certain words with a mockney accent which drove his father to distraction.

When Prince Charles was born Buckingham Palace was issued with a ration book to secure him a supply of free orange juice and cod-liver oil.

After his son the Prince of Wales tore the felt on a table playing billiards George V banned him from playing for a year.

The Queen won't eat oysters, garlic or snails, while Prince Charles dislikes red wine and doesn't drink coffee.

Having married during the postwar austerity years the Queen and Prince Philip were sent more than 30,000 food parcels from America.

ROYAL WEDDING SLIP-UPS

George IV was so shocked at the physical appearance of the woman he was expected to marry that, clapping eyes on Caroline of Brunswick for the first time, he called his man for a large brandy.

Caroline later complained that, horribly drunk, he had insisted she smoke a pipe in bed on their wedding night. She later attempted to get her own back by sticking pins in a wax effigy of him before throwing this into the fire.

When Augusta of Saxe-Coburg married Frederick, Prince of Wales in 1736 she was sick down her dress. (An ill omen, of course, as he died without ever coming to the throne.)

The Archbishop of Canterbury's sermon at Edward VII's wedding was so boring that the orchestra started tuning up before he had finished.

During their marriage ceremony at St Paul's, Lady Diana Spencer mistakenly called her husband Philip instead of Charles.

At her own wedding the Queen's bouquet went missing, and was eventually discovered in a refrigerator where it had been put by a helpful footman who wished to keep it fresh.

On the same day, serving as a page boy, Prince Michael of Kent who was charged with carrying the bride's train tripped and fell over.

Anne of Cleves' unfortunate nickname, the Flanders Mare, was given her by Henry VIII who was seriously disappointed that she did not look more like her official portraits. 'God be praised', he said later, after hearing of her demise, 'the old harridan is dead.'

Somewhat more forgiving, Charles I insisted after his own nuptials that 'you can get used to anyone's face in a week'.

PECULIAR PRINCELY POSSESSIONS & PRIVILEGES

You may be surprised to learn that Prince Philip has a certificate naming him as a 'qualified boiler trimmer', apparently granted after he took over from Chinese stokers who had deserted the Royal Navy in its hour of need.

As Duke of Cornwall Prince Charles owns HM Prison Dartmoor, and has the right to claim the cargo of any ship wrecked off the Cornish coast.

The Prince also automatically becomes the legal owner of any whale or porpoise washed up on beaches in the duchy.

Prince Andrew has a pink wooden elephant made for him by his older brother when he was at prep school.

In 1948 the newborn Prince Charles was presented with one-and-a-half tons of nappies by the excited people of America.

BIZARRE ROYAL PREROGATIVES

From the reigns of King Charles II to George IV Chelsea's King's Road was a private thoroughfare which only the royal family could use. And even now, a constitutional rather than an absolute monarch, the Queen and her heirs nevertheless still technically retain the right to:

- Declare war on any foreign power.
- Dismiss the government of the day.
- Fire any civil servant she chooses to.
- Sell off the ships of the Royal Navy.
- Disband the Army.
- Give away her sovereign territory to a foreign power.
- Ennoble anyone, or indeed everyone.
- Pardon everyone in gaol, and set them free.

BUCKINGHAM PALACE:
WHAT THE OWNERS THINK OF IT

Buckingham Palace has 775 rooms including 19 state rooms, 52 royal and guest bedrooms, 188 staff bedrooms, 92 offices and 78 bathrooms. Even so Princess Margaret always claimed it was cosy although Queen Victoria – the first monarch actually to live there – complained about the distances from one part to another and found the whole place 'so fatiguing'.

Edward VII similarly thought it a sepulchre (he didn't much like Balmoral either, which he described as 'the Highland Barn of a Thousand Draughts'), while George VI found the palace 'like an ice box' and Edward VIII complained about its 'dank, musty smell'.

Prince Philip, who first referred to the royal family as 'the firm', similarly described Buckingham Palace as 'not ours. It's a tied cottage.'

SOME STRANGE ATTENDANTS
ON THE ROYAL HOUSEHOLD

The Lord of the Manor of Scrivelsby is the official Queen's Champion and since William the Conqueror's day has been charged with presenting himself at Westminster before each coronation. He is there in order literally to throw down the gauntlet on the monarch's behalf and thus to do battle with anyone present who wishes to contest his or her accession to the throne. The Dymoke family of Lincolnshire has held this gauntlet – and the associated honour – since 1350.

England's original Hereditary Grand Falconer of England was the first Duke of St Albans, the natural son of Charles II and Nell Gwynn, who also enjoyed the hitherto uniquely regal privilege of being able to ride along Birdcage Walk. Until 1828 he was the only non-member of the royal family permitted to do so.

Three centuries later this office is still in his family, although in 1953 Osborne de Vere Beauclerk (1875–1964), 12th Duke of St Albans, Earl of Burford, Baron Vere of Hanworth and of Heddington – 'Obby' to his pals – boycotted the Queen's coronation because palace officials refused him leave to enter Westminster Abbey with a live falcon on his arm and suggested he wear a stuffed bird instead.

The High Almoner, traditionally a bishop, still wears a towel at his waist as a reminder to Christian kings to follow the example of Christ and to echo His humility in washing the feet of others at the Last Supper. Elizabeth I was a great fan of this, but concerns over the generally low standard of hygiene displayed by the masses meant that actual foot-washing came to an end with King George II in 1730.

The office of the Lord Great Chamberlain – one uniquely shared between three families, who take turns as a new monarch ascends the throne – has been in existence since Norman times. In return for various minor ceremonial duties the holder is entitled to demand anything the sovereign wears at a coronation (including undergarments), also his or her bed, and the throne. The present holder is the Marquess of Cholmondeley with Lord Carrington's family and the Earl of Ancaster's currently awaiting their next turn.

Barges no longer provide the quickest way to travel from the palace at Hampton Court to Westminster or to Greenwich – although the way things are going that could change – but when the Crown Jewels travel by carriage they traditionally do so in the company of the Queen's Bargemaster and the Royal Watermen.

KEEPING 'THE FIRM' ON THE MOVE

Although these days the Royal Mews contain more motor cars than horse-drawn carriages, the monarch retains the services of a Master of Horse as they have done since the time of Edward III and the Siege of Calais.

Her Majesty Queen Elizabeth II famously travels around London in a car with no number plate – and is the only person in the kingdom permitted to do this. She does have one though, JGY 280, which was attached to the car given to her by George VI on her eighteenth birthday and which she still has today.

Somewhat surprisingly Her Majesty is also an accomplished train driver, having taken the controls in Canada and South Africa on a number of occasions and driven an engine named after her from its shed in Swindon to a nearby station platform.

Prince Philip is credited with the idea in 1951 of fixing royal limousines with a plexiglass 'bubble roof' in order that the public can better see Her Majesty. Despite an equerry telling the queen that sitting in such a vehicle she looked like an orchid wrapped in cellophane, the practice has continued.

In 1863 Queen Victoria's carriage was overturned by a drunken coachman. In Her Majesty's own words, she was 'precipitated to the ground' and sustained a black eye.

After the Wall Street crash, Buckingham Palace ordered an additional five Daimler Double-Six limousines to help unemployment in the Midlands.

A white Mercedes 600 made an unwelcome appearance at the office of the Orders of Knighthood behind Buckingham Palace in 1969: it was John Lennon returning the insignia of his MBE.

Edward VIII became a firm fan of Lanchester cars, but in 1919 his father George V dismissed the company's new Forty model as 'more suited to a prostitute than a prince'.

During a demonstration of his company's latest TRX prototype for Princess Margaret at the 1950 Motor Show, Triumph chairman Sir John Black accidentally pulled the wrong lever and incinerated the car.

In 1957 while driving off in his Lagonda after giving a speech about the importance of road safety, the Duke of Edinburgh ploughed into another vehicle which emerged without warning from a side street.

In October 1967 Prince Charles, a brand new undergraduate, arrived at Trinity College, Cambridge, in a red, chauffeur-driven Mini.

Thirty years later royal-watchers were stunned to read in the race programme that Prince Charles had entered the Monaco Grand Prix driving a Maserati. In fact it turned out to be a misprint, the driver in question being somebody by the name of Charles Prince.

Princess Margaret once owned an unusual black convertible Nash Metropolitan, but it was stolen by a fourteen year-old schoolboy.

The Queen learned to drive while serving with the ATS during wartime, something which would have appalled her great-grandmother Queen Victoria who thought all motorcars 'shaky and disagreeable conveyances which smell exceedingly nasty'.

Prince Philip's first car was a Standard Nine but he spent much the late 1960s driving the somewhat swisher Ogle Triplex GTS prototype. Years later Princess Anne was caught speeding in a production version of a similar car.

Lord Mountbatten's number plate was LM 0246, the four digits being the peer's ex-directory Mayfair telephone number.

No mere 'flying lady' the Queen has her own personal bonnet mascot, a solid silver figure of St George slaying the dragon, which is fixed to whichever vehicle she is using that day.

The first time the Queen ever went on a tube train was on 15 May 1939. She took her sister Princess Margaret along, and they sat next to a charlady who had travelled in from Muswell Hill.

That same month, rarely if ever ruffled, the princesses' grandmother Queen Mary emerged without a hair out of place when her Daimler overturned after being hit by a scaffolding truck.

Something of a privilege, one of Prince Andrew's driving instructors was Formula One World Champion Graham Hill. Prior to this his first car had been a pedal-powered Aston Martin toy. Costing a hefty £4,000, it came equipped with many of the gadgets James Bond employed in the 007 film *Goldfinger*.

FLYING THE FLAG

The Union Flag is to be flown officially from all Government and public buildings in the capital on the following days:

20 January	Countess of Wessex's birthday
6 February	Anniversary of the Queen's accession to the throne
19 February	Duke of York's birthday
10 March	Earl of Wessex's birthday
21 April	HM Queen's birthday
23 April	St George's Day
9 May	Europe Day
2 June	Coronation Day
10 June	Duke of Edinburgh's birthday
15 August	Princess Royal's birthday
14 November	Prince of Wales's birthday
20 November	Queen's wedding anniversary

Flags are also flown for the opening and prorogation of Parliament, and on changing dates in March, June and November for Commonwealth Day, the Queen's official birthday, and Remembrance Sunday. Should the Flag of St George also be flown at the same time from an adjacent pole, it is correctly never flown higher than the Union Flag.

ROYAL SALUTES

Ceremonial guns sound over London on each of the following occasions:

> HM Queen's accession day
> HM Queen's birthday
> Coronation Day
> The Duke of Edinburgh's birthday
> The Queen's official birthday
> The State Opening of Parliament

Royal births are also marked in this manner, along with those occasions when visiting Heads of State are presented to the Queen.

On the day of an official salute six 13-pounders from the First World War (pulled by half a dozen horses at full gallop) arrive on the exercise ground in Hyde Park where they are rapidly assembled by the men of the King's Troop, Royal Horse Artillery. Named as such only since 1947, the troop retains its Victorian uniform of blue tunics with yellow frogging, red-striped breeches and bearskins with red bags and white plumes.

A 'basic' royal salute is twenty-one rounds with an additional twenty being fired at Hyde Park because it is a royal park. By the same token on royal anniversaries a full sixty-two rounds are discharged at the Tower, this being the basic twenty-one plus twenty because it is a royal palace with a further twenty-one rounds being discharged 'for the City of London'. Exceptional 101-gun salutes also mark the moment the crown is placed on the head of a new sovereign.

Salutes fired from the Tower are discharged from Second World War 25-pounders, and here the honour of lighting the blue touchpaper goes to members of the Honourable Artillery Company. The City's own territorial unit, this is the oldest military body in the United Kingdom with its origins dating back to a company of sixteenth-century archers known as the Guild of St George.

On Remembrance Sunday a single shot is fired on Horse Guards' Parade to signal the beginning of the traditional two minutes' silence at 11am, with another being discharged precisely 120 seconds later.

FIVE FANTASTICALLY UNROYAL LONDON MOMENTS

Prince Andrew was once caught sledging down the stairs at Buckingham Palace on a valuable silver salver.

Discovering that palace guards had to present arms each time she passed, Princess Anne spent much of her youth rushing up and down in front of them before being told to stop it by her parents.

Skating on thin ice in the grounds of Buckingham Palace, the normally highly composed Prince Albert fell into the lake.

Before going into exile James II somewhat petulantly threw the Great Seal into the River Thames.

When the conductor Sir Landon Ronald was conducting the orchestra playing the National Anthem Edward VII was once heard to snap at him 'Hurry it up, man!'

A CORNER OF A FOREIGN FIELD: ENGLISH ROYALTY BURIED ABROAD

William the Conqueror died of burst bowels after falling from his horse and is buried at Abbey of St Stephen, Caen.

Richard the Lionheart, Henry II, Eleanor of Aquitaine and Isabella of Angoulême are all buried at Fontrêvaud.

Philip II of Spain, who despite his relative youth married England's Mary I, is buried at El Escorial.

James II, to his everlasting shame the only English king to be succeeded by his daughter while he was still alive, was buried in Paris and later removed to St Germain-en-Laye.

And George I, the last actual foreigner to accede to the English throne, is buried at Herrenhausen.

THE KING'S HEAD & OTHER MISSING BODY PARTS

Charles I's neck vertebrae, sliced through by the executioner's axe, disappeared and was only recovered hundreds of years later when an understandably horrified Queen Victoria discovered it being used as a salt cellar by her Royal Surgeon, Sir Henry Halford.

Catherine de Valois, Henry V's wife, suffered the indignity of being dug up and having her corpse put on public display. It remained on show for more than 200 years, Pepys recording having kissed it on the lips for a shilling.

For a long while it was possible to touch Richard II's jaw through a hole in his coffin and (perhaps unsurprisingly) it was eventually stolen by a schoolboy. That was in 1776 and it remained on the missing list until 1906 when the child's descendants finally decided to return it.

The body of Henry IV is thought to have been thrown overboard by superstitious sailors during a storm off the coast of Kent. When his coffin was opened in 1832, a substitute corpse is said to have been discovered dressed in common clothes.

History has not been kind to Richard III, and nor on occasion have his subjects. Originally buried in Grey Friars, Leicester, his bones were subsequently dug up and thrown into the waters of the River Soar.

SIXTEEN SURPRISING ROYAL HOBBIES

For a while Prince Philip developed a passion for barbecues and liked to cook his own sausages for breakfast until the Queen complained to him about the smell.

Presumably keen not to disturb the ancient fabric of Windsor or of Buckingham Palace, Edward VII had an American-style bowling alley installed at Sandringham.

The Duke of Edinburgh collects cartoons of himself, including one drawn by his eldest son, and has them hanging in the loo.

Princess Margaret enjoyed crossword puzzles a great deal, and on several occasions won small prizes for them from the magazine *Country Life*.

George VI admitted one of his favourite pastimes was running cine films backwards and apparently particularly enjoyed watching swimmers exit the pool feet first in order to end up on the diving board.

As well as collecting carvings of her many children's hands in marble, Queen Victoria commissioned a similar mini-sculpture of her beloved Prince Albert's 'sweet little ear'.

Victoria was also a demon card-player, and insisted that anyone who lost to her pay up using only newly minted coins. Her skill meant a supply had to be kept at the palace for precisely this purpose.

King George VI was a keen and skilful embroiderer and presented his wife with a dozen petit-point chair covers for her to use at Royal Lodge.

Once a small boy like any other, Prince Charles used to collect plastic toys from cereal packets and would get upset if palace staff refused to open more than one box at a time.

The queen is a keen pigeon fancier and keeps more than 250 racing pigeons, each of which wears a leg-ring stamped with the royal monogram 'ER.'

George III's son Augustus, Duke of Sussex, amassed an immense private library including a collection of more than 5,000 copies of the Bible.

Edward VII so enjoyed watching buildings on fire that he had his own fireman's uniform made in order that he could do so incognito.

The Queen Mother proved herself in public to be adept at both billiards and bongo-drumming.

Prince Albert designed the Balmoral tartan, as well as some royal pigsties.

William IV, Georges IV and VI, and Edwards VII and VIII were all freemasons.

Preferring cricket to horse racing Prince Philip has been known to wear a special top-hat to the race course. Containing a radio receiver, it means he can keep up with the score.

ROYAL CEREMONIAL: SOME STRANGE SURVIVORS . . .

Since the late thirteenth century (and possibly a good deal earlier) a senior judge known as the Queen's Remembrancer presides over the mysteriously named Trial of the Pyx. Once a year a jury of goldsmiths inspects newly minted coins of the realm to ensure they are of the right size and the metal of an appropriate quality.

Although Temple Bar once left for Hertfordshire and has now been re-erected in Paternoster Square, the monarch still stops at its original location on Fleet Street to ask the Lord Mayor for permission to enter the City and to surrender to him the Sword of State.

On 1 March, St David's Day, a member of the royal family is always on hand to make a present of leeks to members of the Welsh Guards. (Speaking of which, to tell one guards regiment from another count the buttons on their scarlet tunics. If these are presented individually he's a Grenadier, in pairs means it means he's Coldstream, in threes a Scots Guard, fours an Irish Guard and fives a Welsh Guard.)

More than 400 years after the infamy of Guido Fawkes, the Yeomen of the Guard are still charged with searching the cellars of the Palace of Westminster before the official Opening of Parliament in order to thwart another Popish plot. These days they are ably assisted by the Met.

Once a year specially minted silver Maundy money is distributed to twice as many old people as the monarch's age in years. An ancient ceremony which dates back to Edward I's time, it was cancelled by James II and not revived until 1932. Disappointingly some of these unique and special coins have found their way on to eBay.

Each Feast of th Epiphany the monarch makes a gift of gold, frankincense and myrrh at the Queen's Chapel at St James's Palace. The actual task of presentation now falls to her Gentlemen Ushers, but until the reign of George III the monarch performed the offering in person.

Marking Charles II's birthday and his successful concealment in an oak tree after the disastrous Battle of Worcester (1651), Oak Apple Day is still marked by Chelsea Pensioners at the Royal Hospital. On 29 May they parade with oak sprigs, deck the king's statue in oak branches, and feast on beer and plum pudding.

. . . AND A FEW WHICH HAVE BEEN ABANDONED

Until the reign of the brandy-loving Queen Anne, whose ankles were deemed to have grown too fat to fit, it was traditional at each new monarch's coronation for a functionary to buckle on a new pair of spurs.

In July 1958 the Queen finally dispensed with the presentation of debutantes at court, and young women wishing to appear well-born were no longer required to wear long white gloves and to curtsey to a large white cake.

Up to but excluding Queen Victoria's funeral in 1901 the last rites of British monarchs were traditionally held after dark.

Following Prince Philip's declaration that it was unmanly to do so royal footmen at Buckingham Palace no longer powder their hair.

From 1849 until 1957 anyone giving birth to triplets was sent three guineas from the royal household accounts.

Until Edward VIII changed the rules in 1936, Beefeaters at the Tower of London were required to wear beards.

END OF AN ERA

King Charles I was the last monarch ever to enter the chamber of the House of Commons.

In 1952 the Queen curtsied for the very last time, to the coffin of her late father George VI.

George III was technically the last King of America, also the last to insist he was the King of France. (Queen Elizabeth the Queen Mother was similarly the last Empress of India.)

William IV was the last king ever to dismiss his government, although all subsequent monarchs have in principle been free to do so.

William IV was also the last monarch to be buried at night time.

Princess Margaret's was the last royal birth to be witnessed by the Secretary of State, something which had been a somewhat intrusive legal requirement since the reign of Queen Anne.

Unjustly reviled, Richard III was the last English king to die in battle.

By contrast George II, while the last king to lead his troops into battle, died somewhat ingloriously sitting on the loo. (Dead at 77, he was the last English king to be born on foreign soil.)

As for Charles II, he took so long to pass away after having a stroke that he actually apologised to his courtiers for being 'an unconscionable time a-dying'.

3

STREETS, SQUARES & SUBWAYS

A TO Z OF STRANGE STREET NAMES

Ascalon Street, SW8: Named after the Biblical town of Ashequelon, where Samson slayed the Philistines.

Bleeding Heart Yard, EC1: Almost certainly derived from an ancient religious symbol, later adopted by a medieval tavern which once stood on this site.

Crutched Friars, EC3: Crutched is an old form of 'crossed', denoting the order of the Friars of the Holy Cross who were active in nearby Hart Street.

Dog Kennel Hill, SE22: Occupies the site of kennels kept by Prince George of Denmark. (Compensation, perhaps, for his wife Queen Anne declining to make him king.)

Electric Avenue, SW9: One of the first streets in the capital to be lit by electricity, specifically to facilitate late-night shopping.

French Ordinary Court, EC2: An 'ordinary' being an eating house, this one dates back to 1670 and serving local French ex-pats.

Glasshouse Street, W1: Not as nice as it sounds, being a site where saltpetre for glass-making was extracted from domestic effluence collected from the surrounding houses.

Ha Ha Road, SE18. A development built over former parkland on which this particular feature would have been found.

Idol Lane, EC3. Formerly 'Idle Lane', possibly denoting an area of the city where loiterers would congregate.

Jewry Street, EC3. Originally 'Poor Jewry', to distinguish the local Jewish community from the better-off one round the corner at Old Jewry.

Kennington Oval, SE11: Against expectations the cricket ground's distinctive shape was dictated by the layout of the surrounding streets rather than the other way round.

Lizard Street, EC1: Built on land owned by the Worshipful Company of Ironmongers whose coat of arms incorporates two salamanders.

Minories, EC3: The Sorores Minores (or Little Sisters) established a convent here in 1293. The church with which they were associated was only demolished in 1958.

Newington Butts, SE11: Newington means 'new village', with Butts referring to an odd scrap of land possibly used for archery practice.

Ogle Street, W1. Built on land formerly belonging to the dukes of Portland, one of whose subsidiary titles was Baron Ogle.

Pickle Herring Street, SE1. A wharf close by was for many years associated with cargoes of this particular delicacy.

Quex Road, NW6: Refers to Quex Park, the country estate of local Kilburn landowners, the Powell-Cottons.

Rotten Row, SW7: An unfortunate corruption of Route de Roi, the king's road. Equipped with oil lamps for William III it was the first lit thoroughfare in England.

Shrapnel Close, SE18: Commemorates Henry Shrapnel, inventor of the lethally-effective fragmentation shell.

Thermopylae Gate, E14: Named after the fast clipper of this name, built in 1868 and sunk in 1907. As the record books show, only the *Cutty Sark* could rival her astonishing performance.

Undershaft, EC3: A maypole or shaft was erected nearby, but its use then banned for many years after the 1571 May Day Riots.

Verulam Place, WC1: The scholar Francis Bacon, Baron Verulam and Viscount St Albans, kept chambers at nearby Grays Inn from 1597 to 1626.

Wardrobe Place, EC4: From 1359 until it burned down in the Great Fire, royal ceremonial clothes were stored in a house acquired for this purpose within the City walls.

XX Place, E1. Now sadly demolished, although its existence is still commemorated in the name of a Bromley-by-Bow health centre close to its original location.

Yorkshire Grey Yard, WC1. Another name derived from a former inn, referring to the well-known breed of horse.

Zoar Street, SE1. A Baptist chapel stood nearby, Zoar being a place of sanctuary in the New Testament.

TEN BARMY BUT UNREALISED
DEVELOPMENT SCHEMES

In 1815 an Irish MP, Colonel Sir Frederick Trench, lobbied for months to build a giant pyramid designed to cover the whole of Trafalgar Square.

Ten years later Sir Frederick drew up plans for an immense new royal palace, approached along an avenue several hundred feet wide and which, stretching from Hyde Park to St Paul's, would have required the demolition along the way of Covent Garden, the Crusaders' ancient Temple Church and much of the West End.

In 1875 musical impresario Colonel J.H. Mapleson spent a whopping £103,000 on a new opera house with its own underground station, a tunnel connecting it to the Houses of Parliament, even a billiard room and Turkish baths for the performers. But unfortunately he couldn't raise the last £10,000 needed to complete the roof and after £3,000 was spent demolishing it New Scotland Yard was built over the site and the rozzers moved in.

In the 1880s John Leighton seriously suggested redrawing the boundaries of every London borough so that each one would be hexagonal. His reasoning was that this would make it harder for dishonest cab drivers to cheat on their fares.

Even more bizarrely, in 1796 a House of Commons Committee spent several days considering a barely credible plan to straighten out the River Thames. The scheme's sponsor, Willey Reveley, proposed to dig a new channel nearly a mile long in order to save ships the time wasted sailing round the Isle of Dogs.

That most respected engineer Robert Stephenson also dipped his toes into the waters of the Thames, approving plans for the Thames Viaduct Railway which, using a giant latticework of steel, would have enabled trains to run down the centre of the river.

Several equally eminent Victorian authorities also favoured a scheme to dam the river at Woolwich, thereby making of the Thames a giant inner-city freshwater lake.

In 1861 an architect called Harry Newton suggested building a pair of massive mid-stream islands in central London in order to accommodate new government offices, the Central Law Courts and some private luxury apartments. The huge cost sank the scheme.

The same year the Liberal parliamentarian Acton Ayrton tabled a proposal to pull down Henry VIII's 'goodly manor', the by-then 350-year-old St James's Palace, in order to build a new university on the site.

In 1918 architect Philip Tilden designed a monumental tower for retail magnate Gordon Selfridge to put on top of his famous store. Unfortunately it was so tall and so heavy that it would almost certainly have squashed the whole thing flat.

THE SIX ROMAN CITY GATES, AND WHERE THEY WERE

Aldgate: Heading out to the east of England and the Romans' first capital at Colchester. Once home to Geoffrey Chaucer, the gate was taken down in 1761 and briefly rebuilt at Bethnal Green. Its original location is at the intersection of Aldgate and Duke's Place.

Bishopsgate. The start of Ermine Street running out towards Lincoln and the north, and rebuilt several times, the final structure was demolished in 1760 but would have stood on modern Bishopsgate opposite Camomile Street.

Cripplegate. The origins of the name still obscure, a fifteenth-century replacement fell victim to a road-widening scheme in 1760 having stood at the end of Wood Street. The materials were sold to a carpenter in nearby Coleman Street, Mr Blagden paying £91 for the right to cart the whole thing away.

Aldersgate. Possibly an afterthought (Moorgate too came much later) and almost certainly linking up with Watling Street running north-west through modern Edgware. The gate was rebuilt and improved in 1670 but taken down ninety years later. Its position has been identified as being opposite 62 Aldersgate Street.

Newgate. On the road to such important towns as Silchester, Bath and Cirencester, and the last to go in 1767, the gate stood on Newgate Street, west of Warwick Lane, and served as a gaol during the reign of Henry II.

Ludgate. Leading out of the city to a burial ground now covered by Fleet Street, the gate was named after the mythical King Lud, traditionally held to be its builder. Demolished in 1760 it would have stood on Ludgate Hill, opposite St Martin's Church.

UNDERWORLD: A SECRET CITY

The Bank of England's building in Threadneedle Street has so many rooms excavated below ground level that its basements, vaults and cellars are actually more spacious than the whole of the former NatWest Tower, Britain's second tallest building.

Beneath the government buildings between Great George Street and King Charles Street another massive complex of more than 200 underground offices extends over some 6 acres. A secret wartime installation, the giveaway is the ground floor (clearly visible from Horse Guards Road) which has been infilled with concrete to a depth of 17ft.

Still strictly off-limits to the public, a network of tunnels connects this vast subterranean citadel to other government administration facilities in Marsham Street and in the Ministry of Defence on the other side of Whitehall. It possibly even reaches into the cellars of Buckingham Palace, although this has never been confirmed, but of course the network became redundant immediately the Soviets exploded their own H-bomb.

BT also has more than 12 miles of Cold War-era tunnels running beneath central London. Officially these are used to run communications cables around central London but they are clearly capable of much more as each is 16ft in diameter and once contained miniature trains to haul the cables. Those known about run from Waterloo to Trafalgar Square and Blackfriars, with other routes running as far west as Shepherd's Bush and as far east as Bethnal Green.

Harrods, with more than 200 departments spread over an incredible 20 acres of floorspace, is another place which extends deep underground. With a private artesian well and a subterranean lock-up for shoplifters, its own tunnel system incorporates wine-cellars, storage space and staff access points before running beneath Brompton Road to emerge in Trevor Place.

When the Metropolitan Board of Works solicited ideas in the 1850s for dealing with London's growing sewage problem the one woman among 140 respondents suggested laying sewers beneath London in a pattern based on the spokes of a wheel. In this way, she said, London's waste could be efficiently transported to the suburbs and sold to farmers at little shops positioned at the end of each pipe.

With all but one of them lying far below the Northern Line, eight massive deep-level shelters were excavated during the Second World War and are still there now. Each comprises twin parallel tunnels an incredible 1,200ft long with sufficient capacity to house 8,000 individuals in organised dormitories. Their locations can be gauged by looking out for the strangely anonymous bunkers at Belsize Park, Goodge Street, Clapham North, Common and South, and Stockwell. The remaining two are beneath Chancery Lane and Camden Town.

Bizarrely the Clapham South shelter was later used to house the first ever Jamaican immigrants, who arrived in 1948 on the *Empire Windrush*, while the one at Chancery Lane has been redeployed as a vast telephone exchange. The British Library turned down the opportunity to use the fire-damaged Goodge Street tunnels as a book repository, but several episodes of *Dr Who* were filmed beneath Camden Town.

The most stylish wartime bunker, however, was almost certainly the Café de Paris in Coventry Street, with its elegant *Lusitania*-style ballroom. Said to be bomb-proof, and hugely popular with the *demi-monde*, it unfortunately received a double direct hit on 8 March 1941 and more than eighty partygoers were killed.

At about this same time, instead of being opened to the public, a new 3-mile stretch of Central Line tunnel from Gants Hill to Leytonstone was handed over to Plessey which used it as a vast, underground factory for assembling aircraft components.

London's oldest commercial safety-deposit facility opened near the Silver Vaults on Chancery Lane in 1882. Client confidentiality naturally means the contents of the many thousands of safety-deposit boxes remain a secret, but when several had to be opened after the vaults flooded in the 1940s the most intriguing item discovered in one of them was a pair of frilly, pre-war knickers to which was attached a label reading, 'My Life's Undoing'.

The huge crypt of St Stephen's Walbrook was literally lost for several centuries. When it was rediscovered in the mid-1960s by the Revd Chad Varah he had it converted into the call centre for his newly established Samaritans organisation.

The modern theatre ticket booth in Leicester Square conceals a vast electricity substation. Immense transformers three storeys down reduce the National Grid's 132,000 volt power supply and distribute it throughout theatreland, east to Covent Garden and to the lighting displays in Piccadilly Circus.

Twice as long as the Channel Tunnel, deeper than most of the tube lines and with a daily capacity of more than 300,000,000 gallons, London's vast Water Ring Main is 50 miles long, wide enough to run a train through. It could theoretically fill the Royal Albert Hall in under three hours.

LONDON'S SEVEN STRANGEST BASEMENTS

Farringdon Lane, EC1. Visible through the lower windows of a lawyers' office at No. 16 is the original medieval 'Clerks' Well' from which Clerkenwell takes its name.

Magpie Alley, EC4. Behind the anonymous office block at 65 Fleet Street can be seen the carefully preserved, fourteenth-century crypt from a religious house founded by the Carmelite Order of White Friars.

Park Place, SW1. Pratt's, one of London's oldest and most exclusive gentlemen's clubs (and since the 1930s the personal possession of the Duke of Devonshire) is hidden away in a basement of an ordinary-looking house just south of Piccadilly.

Park Street, SE1. Demolished as early as 1605, the remains of the Rose, the oldest theatre on Bankside, are preserved in the basement of a 1990s office block.

Russia Row, EC2. While the little-known Wood Street Compter (pronounced 'counter', meaning a gaol) was demolished in the early nineteenth century, several cells from its dungeons still exist and are used for storage by the shops above.

St James's Street, SW1: Dug out over more than three centuries the huge cellars of Berry Brothers & Rudd's famous wine shop extend as far down the street as Pall Mall and at 8,000sq. ft have space for more than 240,000 bottles of port, wine and brandy.

Whitehall, SW1. Popularly known as Henry VIII's Wine Cellar, but actually a remnant of Cardinal Wolsey's palace, in the 1950s this vaulted undercroft – a 40,000cu. ft cavern weighing some 800 tons – was moved more than 40ft in order to preserve it during the rebuilding of Whitehall.

VISITORS WELCOME: HISTORY ON SHOW

Owned and administered by English Heritage and National Trust, Greater London has an impressively wide range of historic properties which are regularly open to the public. Ranging from Roman burial mounds to the Modernist dwelling of iconic emigré architect Erno Goldfinger, they also include a surprising number of stately homes.

Barking: Eastbury Manor House (sixteenth-century)

Bexley: Red House (nineteenth-century)

Camden: Fenton House (seventeenth-century); Kenwood House (eighteenth-century); 2 Willow Road (twentieth-century)

Greenwich: Eltham Palace (fifteenth/twentieth-century); Ranger's House (eighteenth-century)

Hackney: Sutton House (sixteenth-century)

Hounslow: Chiswick House; Osterley Park & House (both eighteenth-century)

Kensington & Chelsea: Carlyle's House (eighteenth-century); Lindsay House (seventeenth-century)

Kingston: Coombe Conduit (sixteenth-century)

Morden: Morden Hall Park (seventeenth-century, with Roman burial mounds)

Richmond: Ham House (seventeenth-century); Marble Hill House (eighteenth-century)

Southwark: George Inn (seventeenth-century); Winchester Palace (thirteenth-century)

Tower Hamlets: London Wall (second-century)

Westminster: Apsley House (eighteenth-century); Blewcoat School (eighteenth-century); Chapter House (thirteenth-century) and Pyx

Chamber (eleventh-century) – both at Westminster Abbey – Jewel Tower (fourteenth-century); 'Roman' Bath (possibly Roman); Wellington Arch (nineteenth-century).

BITS OF LONDON WHICH AREN'T WHERE THEY SHOULD BE

Everyone knows the last London Bridge was sold to the Americans for $2.5 million, and that it can be seen at Lake Havasu City, Arizona. Parts of the one which preceded it, however, have remained closer to home with some of the stonework incorporated into Adelaide House, King William Street and 49 Heathfield Road, SW18. Two stone alcoves have also popped up in Victoria Park, Hackney, with a third one installed in the courtyard of Guys Hospital.

When a pub near Romford called the Mawney Arms was closed for refurbishment in 1999 the interior was stripped out and together with the original pub sign shipped off to Thailand and rebuilt in Koh Samui.

In 1672 a statue of Charles II, mounted and trampling Cromwell underfoot, was removed from the 'Stocks Market' in the City to make way for the new Mansion House. It is now to be seen in Ripon, Yorkshire, although Cromwell, curiously, sports a turban, the statue having been modified from one depicting a Polish king crushing a marauding Turk.

When the Prince Regent's lavish palace at Carlton House was demolished in the 1820s columns from it were incorporated into the façade of the National Gallery and also in the chapel at Buckingham Palace. Some heraldic stained glass was also reused at Windsor Castle.

Following the deliberate destruction of St Antholin's (widely regarded as one of Wren's masterworks) the steeple was removed to south-east London where it forms the centrepiece to an uninspiring 1960s housing estate.

All Hallows, Lombard Street – another Wren design, later deemed superfluous to requirements by the City authorities – was rebuilt as All Hallows, Twickenham. Bizarrely the rebuilding also incorporated the porch from Clerkenwell's Priory of St John.

At least when Wren's St Mary the Virgin Aldermanbury church was gutted by fire, the whole building was kept together. Eventually its more than 7,000 pieces of masonry were shipped to the USA before being reassembled at Fulton, Missouri. Now the chapel of Westminster College, it is a memorial to Sir Winston Churchill who, on a trip to Fulton in 1946, made his landmark speech about an 'iron curtain' descending across Europe.

Damaged by the IRA and swept away to make way for the Gherkin (this despite its Grade II-listed status) the old Baltic Exchange was dismantled piece by piece, and is stored in a barn in Kent. Dismantling it cost an estimated £4,000,000 but it is now for sale for approximately £750,000 to anyone who fancies building themselves a truly unique new-old country house.

Twickenham's decorative Egyptian-style Kilmorey Mausoleum, in which the sock-loathing 2nd Earl of Kilmorey (1787–1880) is said to be buried wearing a dressing gown of rats' fur, was originally erected in Brompton Cemetery. It reputedly cost £30,000 at a time when a matchgirl could reasonably expect to make less than 10s a week, which goes some way to explain why the earl took it with him each time he moved house.

To celebrate the defeat of Napoleon, the Prince Regent had John Nash draw up plans for a splendid, polygonal rotunda to stand in the gardens of Carlton House where he wished to entertain the assembled monarchs of Europe. Once the festivities were over, the Grade II-listed building was dismantled and given to the Royal Regiment of Artillery which rebuilt it as a museum in Repository Road, SE18.

Crosby Hall in Chelsea, now almost certainly London's largest private home, was originally built in the 1460s on Bishopsgate in the City but was rescued and removed brick by brick when threatened with demolition in 1908.

Finally quite a lot of bits of the Royal Observatory at Greenwich should actually be at Tilbury in Essex. The reason they are not is that Sir Christopher Wren, in a bid to economise, recycled a great quanitity of lead, stone and brick from the historic fort there in order to minimise the final bill at Greenwich.

TEN CASTLES IN LONDON

Astor Castle, Temple Place, WC2
William Waldorf Astor's stone-built estate office, the lavish headquarters of his UK business empire, was designed by J. Loughborough Pearson and completed in 1895 in an attractive Early Elizabethan style.

Bruce Castle, Lordship Lane, E17
More of a manor house, Elizabethan, but said to have been built on the remains of Robert the Bruce's castle. It was at one point a private school (run by Rowland Hill, instigator of the penny post) and now houses a library, two museums and the historic collections of the Middlesex Regiment.

Buttress Castle, Phipps Bridge Road, SW19
A charming rustic stone folly, a ruined tower imaginatively conceived to shore up a small terrace of cottages under threat from flooding twice a year from the River Wandle. Now in the care of the National Trust.

Castle Baynard, Blackfriars, EC4
Originally built for a cohort of the Conqueror, Bairnardus or Baynard, and later a royal property, it was home to three of the wives of Henry VIII. Lady Jane Grey and Mary Tudor were both proclaimed Queen here, but after the Great Fire just one turret remained. This was finally taken down in 1720.

Jack Straw's Castle, North End Road, NW3
A famous Hampstead landmark, reputedly built over the spot where the Peasants' leader sought refuge, it was rebuilt in the 1960s by Raymond Erith. Actually a pub, and never a particularly good one, it was converted forty years later into flats.

Pirate's Castle, Oval Road, NW1
A nautically inclined youth club was founded forty years ago by Jestyn Reginald Austen Plantagenet Phillips, 2nd Viscount St Davids. In 1977 it finally moved into a permanent home, this compact but chunky canalside castle was designed for it by the hugely prolific architect Colonel Richard Seifert.

Pomfret Castle, Arlington Street, SW1
In 1760 the Countess of Pomfret commissioned Sanderson Miller to build her a vast Gothic folly in the heart of the West End. Complete with gatehouse, turrets and elaborate plasterwork, it stood alongside an ordinary Georgian terrace. Unfortunately it was demolished in the early twentieth century.

Stoke Newington Castle, Green Lanes, N4
A disused water pumping station modelled by its Victorian creator William Chadwell Mylne on Stirling Castle, this formidable structure has been remodelled inside to provide facilities for fairweather mountaineers as an indoor climbing centre.

Trobridge's Castle, Buck Lane, NW9
Mindful that an Englishman's home was his castle, developer Ernest Trobridge made a fortune building churches and spent it constructing castellated blocks of flats in this otherwise unremarkable north London suburb.

Vanbrugh Castle, Maze Hill, SE10

The first to put a nostalgic spin on architecture, in 1717 Sir John Vanbrugh built himself a miniature medieval fortress for a home, kickstarting a fashion which has never really abated. Happily his castle survives, but is now divided into flats.

MINOR ARCHITECTURAL ODDITIES
NOBODY NOTICES

Architecture, the name given to one of the monumental bronze female figures on Vauxhall Bridge, is holding in her hands a miniature representation of St Paul's Cathedral.

The classical god standing atop the spire of St George's, Bloomsbury, is actually a representation of King George I, the spire itself being modelled on a mausoleum described at length by Pliny.

A stained-glass window at St Mary's New Church, N16, includes an image of the radio telescope at Jodrell Bank.

The weathervane on the Royal Exchange in the City is a grasshopper not a cock, the former being the crest of its founder Sir Thomas Gresham.

The scary-looking gargoyles on the façade of the Natural History Museum are in fact a fair representation of the extent of man's palaeontological knowledge at the time the museum was being built.

Affixed to the wall of the Charterhouse on the edge of the City is London's oldest surviving sundial. Dated 1611, it marks the year Thomas Sutton established his famous school.

The splendid mosaic on the south porch of the Royal Albert Hall comprises an incredible 60,000 individual pieces. (And weighing more than 150 tons, the organ inside has 9,779 pipes.)

The light at the top of St Stephen's Tower, Westminster – more popularly known as Big Ben – is lit only when Parliament is in session.

The stone blocks on the pavement outside the Athenaeum in Waterloo Place were originally installed to enable the Duke of Wellington to more easily mount his horse.

The figure of 'the Old Lady of Threadneedle Street' on the façade of the Bank of England has a model of the bank on her lap.

The German Gymnasium by St Pancras station is so named because it was built in 1864 by the German Gymnasium Society for the use of German businessmen travelling to London. On the outbreak of hostilities in 1914, it became a club for railwaymen. In 1866 the National Olympian Association held its first ever Games in the building, and these were repeated every year until the modern Olympics moved in 1908 to White City in West London.

EIGHT GREAT VANISHED MANSIONS

Carlton House, Pall Mall, SW1
Thirty years in the making, the sums involved sufficient almost to sink the monarchy, and depending on your point of view either the equal of Versailles – Horace Walpole called it 'the most perfect palace' – or 'overdone with finery', in the words of architect Robert Smirke. In any event no sooner was it finished than the Prince Regent ascended to the throne, lost interest in it, and in a bid for something even finer, started work on Buckingham Palace. By 1827 the whole thing had been swept away.

Devonshire House, Piccadilly, SW1
William Kent's masterpiece for the 3rd Duke of Devonshire was completed in 1737. An impression of the lifestyle here is suggested by the footmen, who wore epaulettes of solid silver, and the fact

that entertainments featured the Duke's own private orchestra. Torn down in 1924 (it made way for a car showroom also known as Devonshire House) its most conspicuous relic is the large pair of wrought-iron gates into Green Park at the end of Broad Walk.

Dorchester House, Park Lane, W1

The grandest house on one of London's most prestigious thoroughfares, and amazingly it was built for a commoner. Millionaire R.S. Holford's ducal mansion was designed by Louis Vulliamy in 1857 and modelled on Rome's Villa Farnesina. One chimneypiece alone of Carrara marble took 10 years to complete, and the principal staircase cost £30,000. In 1929, however, the house was scheduled for demolition and the staircase knocked down to salvage for just £273 to make way for the hotel of the same name.

Lansdowne House, Berkeley Square, W1

Regarded in the 1780s as one of the great houses of Europe, the palace Robert Adam built for Lord Bute was acquired by the 1st Marquess of Lansdowne before completion. Leased by Gordon Selfridge, in the 1930s it was brutally shorn of its façade to make way for traffic streaming into Fitzmaurice Place. The main drawing room and dining room were preserved, intact, and shipped off to museums in North America while what remained was remodelled for a new 'cock and hen club', the Lansdowne, which has occupied it ever since.

Monmouth House, Soho Square, W1

Little is known about the Duke of Monmouth's Soho mansion besides its staggering dimensions. Clearly a magnificent palace with a frontage of 76ft, a depth of 280ft and extensive stabling and coach houses running along the east side of Frith Street, work began in 1682. The Duke never lived to enjoy it, however. The eldest of Charles II's illegitimate sons, he engaged in rebellion and was beheaded after losing the Battle of Sedgemoor three years later. His battle-cry had been an appropriate shout of 'so-ho'.

Norfolk House, St James's Square, SW1

Occupying a substantial site on the east side of the square, and bought by the 8th Duke of Norfolk in 1722 for the incredible sum of £10,000, it remained in the family for the next eight generations before being sold in 1937. Plain without but glorious within, it was the birthplace of George III and when it was demolished to make way for an office block in 1939 the music room was removed to the Victoria and Albert Museum where it can still be seen.

Northumberland House, Strand, WC2

Squeezed between Trafalgar Square and the Embankment, and hemmed in on every side by a crush of offices and shops, the London home of the dukes of Northumberland somehow survived until 1874: it was the last of the great Strand mansions to succumb. As a memento of their London presence the giant, emblematic Percy lion which stood high above the main gateway for nearly 150 years was removed to Syon House, the dukes' estate at Isleworth.

Somerset House, Strand, WC2

The forerunner of the glittering cultural showplace we have today was England's first renaissance palace. Designed for the Lord Protector the Duke of Somerset, possibly by the celebrated John of Padua, it was Tudor London's finest address. The river frontage was some 600ft, and to build it in 1547–50 stone was pulled from the cloister of St Paul's Cathedral and the Priory Church of St John, Clerkenwell. An attempt was made to plunder more from St Margaret's Westminster, but the workmen were beaten back by the parishioners.

NEWER HOUSES WORTH NOTICING

No. 43 Banstock Road, HA8: What looks at first like a typical half-timbered suburban semiturns out on closer inspection to be a metal prefab, its ingenious design conceived to soak up surplus capacity in the aircraft industry when peace was declared in 1945. The 'half-timbering', complete with winding metal vines, was applied later by an owner presumably keen to advertise his home's unusual construction.

16 Club Row, E2: Showing superb utilisation of a site so small it had been left vacant for nearly half a century, in 2001 Sarah Cheeseman and Howard Carter of the architectural practice Thinking Space squeezed a house on three floors with a roof terrace, two bedrooms and a central atrium on to barely more ground than could have accommodated a single lock-up garage.

Fifteen-and-a-Half Consort Road, SE15: Proof were it needed that the greater the constraints the more imaginative an architect will be, Richard Paxton's house with its opening roof and sliding bath was voted into the top half-dozen of new British houses in a survey on national television.

40 Douglas Road, N1: Its glass-brick frontage providing the starkest possible contrast with the chaste Georgian terraces of the neighbourhood, this 1994 townhouse by Future Systems gets away with it thanks to careful proportions and an elegant sweeping staircase designed to avoid a mature tree growing directly in front of it.

2 Garner Street, E2: Built as a combined home and workplace for architect Sean Griffiths and his wife, this imaginative composition advertises its dual function by being expressly designed to look like a clapboard cottage standing in front of a miniature office block.

24 Helios Road, SM6: The BedZed Project – Beddington Zero Energy – is a development of 100 homes and 10 studios designed to be carbon neutral. Solar-powered, they feature distinctive colourful rooftop cowlings to ensure efficient distribution of air.

52 Mountfield Road, W5: A deceptively large house, built by the owners and squeezed on to a long thin plot, the design incorporates

a striking, double-height glazed courtyard and uses many energy-saving, ecologically sound materials. A breathable external shell keeps the interior warm in winter and cool in summer, and all rain and mains water is efficiently recycled.

10 Stock Orchard Street, N7: Built largely of straw bales, and mounted on sprung, gabion-clad columns to reduce vibrations from an adjacent railway line, Sarah Wigglesworth's eco-friendly home-cum-workspace looks extraordinary but combines both advanced thinking and deeply traditional building methods and materials.

Segal House, Walters Way, SE23: Perhaps providing a solution for the current search for low-cost housing for so-called essential workers, in the 1960s Austrian ex-pat architect Walter Segal devised a simple, flat-roof design for the home-builder. Functional and affordable, they haven't caught on yet although their creator enjoyed the unique distinction of having two London streets named after him within his lifetime.

LONDINIUM: WHERE TO SEE BITS OF ROMAN LONDON

Literally hundreds of fragments from the Roman city are preserved but concealed beneath more modern developments, but some larger pieces are visible if you know where to look:

All Hallows Barking by the Tower, EC3: a massive Saxon arch at one end of the church has clearly been constructed using Roman tiles and stones from the Roman wall. (The crypt also contains broken pottery from the sacking of the City by Queen Boudicca in AD 60.)

Amphitheatre, EC2: The eastern entrance to this has been preserved beneath the Guildhall and can be viewed from the Art Gallery.

Cripplegate Fort, EC2: A portion of the original second-century stonework (now surmounted by medieval defences) can be clearly seen from the windows of the Museum of London.

Mithraeum, Queen Victoria Street, EC4: The substantial remains of an authentic Roman temple, removed here from Walbrook in the 1950s.

London Wall, EC2: Originally 2 miles in length and enclosing 330 acres of the city, surviving sections can be seen beneath the Wardrobe Tower at the Tower of London, by Tower Hill underground station, and beneath the old Post Office yard in Newgate Street.

Recovery of Londinium by Constantius Chlorus AD 296

Roman Fort, EC1: In the underground car park at London Wall a room contains the remains of the West Gate to this characteristically playing-card-shaped fort, also part of its guardroom which was excavated in 1956/7. Fragments of wall and turret are also partly concealed by undergrowth in the public gardens in Noble Street.

Tesselated Pavement, EC4: St Bride's Church in Fleet Street contains fragments of this while a small portion of timber from a Roman quay is visible in the forecourt of St Magnus Church, Lower Thames Street, EC3.

LONDON'S SURVIVING WINDMILLS

More than forty entries under 'Windmill' in the index of the *London A-to-Z* suggest the original whereabouts of the many windmills which would once have stood in and around London. Today just seven survive, in various states of repair, with at least two regularly coming under attack from vandals.

Old Mill Road, Plumstead, SE18	Windmill Road, Mitcham, CR4
St Mary Lane, Upminster, E17	Windmill Gardens, Brixton, SW2
Upper Shirley Road, Croydon, CR0	Windmill Road, Wandsworth, SW18
Windmill Road, Wimbledon, SW19	

4

MEN, WOMEN & CHILDREN

NOTABLE LONDON ECCENTRICS

Sir Francis Galton (1822–1911)
A eugenics pioneer, Charles Darwin's cousin devised what he called a Beauty Map of Britain. Travelling the country to discover where were the prettiest girls, he eventually concluded that the loveliest were from London and the ugliest in Aberdeen. Surprisingly the map became a best-seller – especially in Aberdeen.

David William Anthony Blyth Macpherson (1924–2006)
Lord Strathcarron, a charming wartime flying-boat pilot, motoring journalist and racing driver, continued competing into his mid-seventies and well past his eightieth birthday was still to be seen leaving his Chelsea home astride a large BMW motorcycle with one of his four wives riding pillion and his beloved parrot Perry bringing up the rear.

Geoffrey Nathaniel Pyke (1894–1948)
A real-life Professor Branestawm with a set in Albany, during the Second World War Pyke almost persuaded the powers-that-be that the future lay in giant battleships made of ice and sawdust. Calling the stuff 'pykrete' he argued it was unsinkable, something his sponsor Lord Mountbatten tried to prove by dropping a lump into Churchill's bath and then shooting it with a revolver. Unfortunately the bullet ricocheted off and hit Admiral King in the leg.

William Francis Brinsley Le Poer Trench (1911–95)
An advertising salesman and founding editor of the *Flying Saucer Review*, Le Poer Trench is distinguished from your average UFO loon by virtue of his seat in the House of Lords where he sat as the 8th Earl of Clancarty. He successfully established an official Parliamentary All-Party UFO Study Group in a bid to prove his pet theory that the majority of UFOs came not from outer space but from secret bases inside the Earth. Believing the planet to be hollow, he insisted there were entrance tunnels at both poles and that he could trace his descent back to 63,000 BC and a race of aliens.

A.D. Wintle (1897–1966)
Born in Russia, schooled in France and educated in Germany, Lt-Colonel Alfred Wintle nevertheless got down on his knees every night of his life 'and thanked God for making me an Englishman'. A career cavalryman in the Royal Dragoons, he sincerely believed time spent anywhere but on the back of a horse was time wasted. Imprisoned as a spy he took his captors to task for their scruffy demeanour, insisting they were unfit to guard an officer in the King's Army. Years later, on ITV's *This is Your Life*, the head of the garrison admitted his men had eventually switched sides 'entirely because of the Colonel's dauntless example and his tirade of abuse and challenge'.

Francis Bacon (1561–1626)
This prolific philosopher, writer and statesman – he was Lord Chancellor under James I – also found time to dabble in science. In the winter of 1626, while out with friends on Highgate Hill, he ordered the coachman to stop, and stepping down into the snow

bought, plucked and disembowelled a chicken before stuffing it with snow. An early experiment in food preservation, the chicken certainly lasted longer – but, sadly, Sir Francis did not. Catching a chill and taking to his bed, he quickly died. The event is marked by Bacons Lane, close to Highgate Cemetery.

Gerald Hugh Tyrwhitt-Wilson (1883–1950)

With rooms in Half Moon Street, the 14th Lord Berners installed a piano in the back of his Rolls-Royce, had the doves on his Berkshire estate dyed red, white and blue, and once invited Lady Betjeman's horse round for tea. It was his passion for building which really put him on the map, however, when his neighbour Admiral Clifton-Browne objected to his 140ft tower on the grounds that it would spoil his view. When Berners pointed out that Clifton-Browne lived so far away he could see it only with a telescope, the old sea-dog indignantly pointed out that being an Admiral he naturally never looked through anything else. Berners won the day, however, and placed a sign at the top of his folly warning 'Members of the public committing suicide from this tower do so at their own risk'.

Woodrow Lyle Wyatt (1918–97)

Clearly another, like Colonel Wintle, who was never happier than when extolling the virtues of being an Englishman 'rather than a chimpanzee or a flea, or a Frenchman or a German', this forthright Fleet Street hack and Chairman of the Tote was once asked by a French hotelier to spell his name and replied, 'W-Y-A-T-T – as in Waterloo, Ypres, Agincourt, Trafalgar, Trafalgar.'

Jeremy Bentham (1748–1832)

The philosopher whose embalmed body is still on display in Bloomsbury at University College proposed installing a network of hollow 'conversation tubes' under London so people in different buildings could speak to each other without going outside. He also thought eminent men should be preserved and stuffed as an example to others, hence his present state. Unfortunately his own head quickly rotted away and has had to be replaced by a wax replica.

HOLLYWOOD BIG HITTERS WHO WERE BORN IN LONDON

Dirk Bogarde	Leslie Howard	Elizabeth Taylor
Charlie Chaplin	Boris Karloff	Bob Hope
Stewart Granger	Angela Lansbury	Peter Ustinov
Alfred Hitchcock	Peter Lawford	

SURPRISING PEOPLE WHO LIVED IN LONDON (& WHERE)

Hector Berlioz (1803–69) 58 Queen Anne Street, W1
Canaletto (1697–1768) 41 Beak Street, W1
Charles de Gaulle (1890–1970) 4 Carlton Gardens, SW1
Mahatma Gandhi (1869–1948) 20 Baron's Court Road, W14
David Ben Gurion (1886–1973) 75 Warrington Crescent, W9
Jimi Hendrix (1942–70) 23 Brook Street, W1
Mohammed Ali Jinnah (1876–1948) 35 Russell Road, W14
Prince Kropotkin (1842–1921) 6 Crescent Road, BR1
Giuseppe Mazzini (1805–72) 183 Gower Street, NW1
Prince Metternich (1773–1859) 44 Eaton Square, SW1
Piet Mondrian (1872–1944) 60 Parkhill Road, NW3
Wolfgang Amadeus Mozart (1756–91)180 Ebury Street, SW1
Napoleon III (1808–73) 1c King Street, SW1
Jawaharlal Nehru (1889–1964) 60 Elgin Crescent, W11

Peter the Great (1672–1725) Sayes Court, SE8
Lucian Pissarro (1863–1944) 27 Stamford Brook Road, W6
Jean-Jacques Rousseau (1712–78) 10 Buckingham Street SW1
Prince Talleyrand (1754–1838) 21 Hanover Square, W1
Mark Twain (1835–1910) 23 Tedworth Square, SW3
Vincent Van Gogh (1853–90) 87 Hackford Road, SW9
Johann Zoffany (1733–1810) 65 Stand-on-the-Green, W4
Emile Zola (1840–1902) 122 Church Road, SE19

A FEW WHO WEREN'T QUITE WHAT THEY SEEMED

The Marquess Montmorenci (1848–1911) was an improbably named racehorse tipster – he was actually born Harry Benson – who amassed a fortune tipping imaginary horses and bribing senior Scotland Yard officers to keep a step or two ahead of the law. They caught him in the end, however, and after securing an early release from a sentence of 15 years' hard labour he fled to the USA, restarted his swindling and died in Tombs Prison, NY.

Jonathan Wild (1689–1725), London's self-styled Thief-taker General, a privateer in an age before there was any organised constabulary, made a mint returning stolen property to its rightful owners and claiming the rewards. Unfortunately much of the property he had stolen himself, or commissioned others to do on his behalf, while also procuring false evidence. After attempting to kill himself with laudanum he was hanged at Tyburn before a cheerful crowd of thousands.

Dr William Dodd (1729–77), founder of the Humane Society for the Relief and Discharge of Small Debtors, soon turned out to be quite a big one himself. Passing a forged cheque drawn on the account of Lord Chesterfield for the then gigantic sum of £4,200 he was found guilty at Newgate and executed.

General James M. Barry (1795–1865), senior Inspector of the Army Medical Department, was revealed at his death to have been a woman. The M clearly standing for Miranda, this means that she was the country's first qualified female doctor, as well of course as the Army's first lady general.

Michael Corrigan (1881–1946) was to all appearances a respectable major in the Brigade of Guards. In this guise Corrigan sold the Tower of London to a stranger, London Bridge at least twice, and the Duke of York's house in Piccadilly to American tourists. Arrested at the Ritz, on being found guilty he hanged himself in Brixton Prison – with his regimental tie, of course.

Lord Gordon-Gordon (1815–73). Conning a London jeweller out of £25,000 and railwayman Jay Gould out of an incredible $1,000,000, in 1873 Gordon-Gordon was caught, jumped bail and fled to Canada. Frustrated in their attempts to extradite him, five of his dupes – including two future State Governers, and three future Congressmen – attempted to kidnap him and ended up in gaol. Gordon-Gordon then threw a massive party to celebrate, sent his guests home with generous gifts and shot himself dead. More than a century later, his true identity has never been discovered.

EVERYBODY ELSE: THE FLUCTUATING POPULATION

The first city anywhere in the world to top a million, and the largest on the planet from 1831 until being overtaken by Tokyo 126 years later, the growth of London has by no means been a one-way street. Figures before 1801 can only be estimated, but historians agree that the population has had its ups and downs. It is known to have collapsed after the withdrawal of Rome, and again during the Black Death. More recently it has been declining steadily, well down from its 1939 peak.

60AD	20,000	1801	959,300
140	45-60,000	1831	1,655,000
300	15-20,000	1851	2,363,000
400	less than 5,000	1891	5,572,012
500	3–400	1901	6,506,954
700	less than 5,000	1911	7,160,525
900	5,000	1921	7,386,848
1000	5–10,000	1931	8,110,480
1100	14-18,000	1939	8,615,245
1300	50,000	1951	8,196,978
1350	25,000	1961	7,992,616
1500	50–75,000	1971	7,452,520
1600	200,000	1981	6,805,000
1650	350,000	1991	6,829,300
1700	550,000	2001	7,322,400
1750	700,000		

LONDON'S AVENUE OF STARS

Bringing a touch of Hollywood glamour to the capital, the London Avenue of Stars was conceived as a walkway through Covent Garden passing by the actors' church of St Paul's. To qualify one had to be from the United Kingdom, Ireland, or a Commonwealth nation but with the selection of names proving as likely to irritate as to delight the stars were removed and the scheme abandoned within barely a year.

Alan Bates
Alan Bennett
Alan Whicker
Albert Finney
Alec Guinness
Alfred Hitchcock
Alicia Markova
Ant and Dec
Anthony Hopkins
Arthur Lowe
The Beatles
The Bee Gees
Benny Hill
Billy Connolly
Bob Geldof
Bob Hope
Brenda Blethyn
Bruce Forsyth
Cary Grant
Charlie Chaplin
Charles Laughton
Chris Tarrant
Christopher Lee
Cilla Black
Cliff Richard
Coronation Street
David Bowie
David Frost
David Jason
David Niven
Diana Rigg
Dirk Bogarde
Edith Evans
Edna Everage

Elizabeth Taylor
Eric Clapton
Eric Sykes
Errol Flynn
Frankie Howerd
Glenda Jackson
Gracie Fields
Harry Secombe
Helen Mirren
Hugh Grant
Ian McKellen
John Cleese
John Gielgud
John Mills
John Thaw
Judi Dench
Julie Andrews
Julie Walters
Ken Dodd
Kenneth Branagh
The Kinks
Kiri Te Kanawa
Laurence Olivier
Lenny Henry
Leonard Rossiter
Les Dawson
Maggie Smith
Margot Fonteyn
Michael Caine
Michael Gambon
Michael Palin
Morecambe & Wise
Nicole Kidman
Nigel Hawthorne

Noel Coward
Paul Eddington
Peggy Ashcroft
Peter Cook
Peter O'Toole
Peter Sellers
Peter Ustinov
Pink Floyd
Queen
Ralph Richardson
Rex Harrison
Richard Attenborough
Richard Briers
Richard Burton
Ricky Gervais
Robbie Coltrane
Robbie Williams
Roger Moore
The Rolling Stones
Rowan Atkinson
Sean Connery
The Sex Pistols
Shirley Bassey
Spike Milligan
Stan Laurel
Thora Hird
Tom Jones
Tommy Cooper
Tony Hancock
Trevor McDonald
The Two Ronnies
Vera Lynn
Victoria Wood
Yehudi Menuhin

RECENT ARRIVALS:
NEW LONDONERS' TOP 20 COUNTRIES OF BIRTH

A recent survey of Londoners estimated that one-third of them had been born overseas, while another looking at London schools found a staggering 307 foreign languages being spoken in the playground. Of these the most common were of South Asian origin: Bengali or Sylheti, Punjabi, Gujerati and Urdu. The rarer ones included Tagalog (Filipino), Akan (Ashanti), Igbo (Nigeria), Pashto (Afganistan) and Mbum (Cameroon).

Country	No. of London residents	% of total
India	172,162	2.4
Eire	157,285	2.2
Bangladesh	84,565	1.2
Jamaica	80,319	1.1
Nigeria	68,907	1.0
Pakistan	66,658	0.9
Kenya	66,311	0.9
Sri Lanka	49,932	0.7
Ghana	46,513	0.6
Cyprus	45,888	0.6
South Africa	45,506	0.6
United States	44,622	0.6
Australia	41,488	0.6
Germany	39,818	0.5
Turkey	39,128	0.5
Italy	38,694	0.5
France	38,130	0.5
Somalia	33,831	0.5
Uganda	32,082	0.4
New Zealand	27,494	0.4

SOME STRANGE STATUE FACTS

The statue of Charles I, incidentally the oldest object in Trafalgar Square, stands on the site of the original Charing Cross and marks the point from which all distances from London are measured.

Carving G.F. Handel's likeness for Westminster Abbey, the great Louis-François Roubiliac objected to the size of the maestro's own ears so replaced them with a smaller pair modelled on those belonging to a young lady.

Landseer similarly copied the forepaws for his famous lions at the foot of the Nelson Column from those attached to a domestic moggie.

The statue known as Eros in Piccadilly circus isn't Eros at all, but rather a memorial to the 7th Earl of Shaftesbury. This is why the young angel (which represents Christian Charity) is shown angling his bow downwards in order to bury the shaft of his arrow.

Although Queen Square, WC1, takes its name from the lead statue of a queen in its centre, no-one knows the sculptor responsible – nor indeed which queen it is meant to represent. Mary, Anne or Charlotte?

In 1702, while riding at Hampton Court, William III was thrown when his horse stumbled on a molehill and subsequently died. This molehill is represented in bronze on his sculpture in the gardens at St James's Square.

The representation of Oliver Cromwell outside Westminster Hall shows him wearing his spurs upside-down. More remarkably still, that of George IV in Trafalgar Square has no spurs whatsoever.

At the Greek Revival St Pancras New Church, WC1, the caryatids made in the likeness of the Athenian Erechtheum were carved to the wrong scale and had to have several inches removed from their midriffs to make them fit.

The statue of Florence Nightingale outside St Thomas's Hospital, SE1, is actually just a glass-fibre replica. The original was stolen in 1970.

The poor, pock-marked condition of General James Wolfe in Greenwich Park, SE10, reflects the damage done to it by a German mine which fell nearby in the 1940s.

Prince Albert lent Thomas Thorneycroft some horses on which to model those being reined in by Queen Boudicca on Victoria Embankment.

The statue of William Huskisson in Pimlico Gardens, SW1, depicts the first person ever to be killed by a train.

The much-derided 40-ton statue of the Duke of Wellington designed to stand on the arch in front of Apsley House but eventually removed to Aldershot, is so ugly that the first Frenchman to see it is said to have cried joyfully, 'We are avenged!'

His Grace, nevertheless, still retains the unique honour of having two equestrian statues of him erected in central London.

The representation of Field Marshal Lord Wolseley in Horse Guards Parade was cast in bronze recycled from captured enemy cannon.

FOREIGNERS DEPICTED ON THE ALBERT MEMORIAL

Commonly assumed to be a typical proud, patriotic monument to great imperial achievement, Prince Albert's famous monument in Kensington Gardens in fact celebrates scores of foreign artists and craftsmen, its frieze of more than 160 figures showing just how internationally minded and outward-looking the Victorians were when it came to those artists whom they held in high esteem. While many are now largely forgotten, and there are some surprising omissions, the continental painters, writers, musicians, composers, architects and sculptors portayed on the memorial outnumber home-grown talent by a factor of more than three to one.

Abbé Suger
Alberti
An. Carracci
Anthemius
Apollodorus
Arnolfo di Lap
Auber
Baccio d'Angelo
Bach
Bandinelli
Beethoven
Bellini
Bernini
Bezaleel
Bontemps
Bramante
Brunelleschi
Bryaxis
Bupulas
Callicrates
Callimachus
Cano
Canova
Carissimi
Cellini
Cervantes
Chares
Cheops
Chersiphron
Cimabue
Claude
Corneille
Correggio
Da Vinci
Dante
David d'Angers
David
Decamps
Delacroix
Delaroche
Delorme
Dibutades
Donatello

Durer
E. Von Steinbach
Fra Angelico
Gerard
Gericault
Ghiberti
Ghirlandaio
Gian di Bologna
Gilliano Di Ravenna
Giotto
Gluck
Goethe
Goujon
Gretry
Guido d'Arezzo
H. Van Eyck
Handel
Haydn
Hermodorus
Hiram
Holbein
Homer
Ictinus
Ingres
Jehan de Chelles
Josqin-des-Pres
L. Carracci
Leochares
Libon
Luca della Robbia
Lulli
Lysippus
Mantegna
Masaccio
Mehul
Mendelssohn
Metagenes
Michaelangelo
Mnesikles
Moliere
Monteverdi
Mozart
Murillo

Nitocris
Orcagna
P. Veronese
Palestrina
Palissy
Palladio
Peruzzi
Phidias
Pilon
Pisano
Poussin
Praxiteles
Puget
Pythagoras
Rameu
Raphael
Rembrandt
Rhoecus
Roubiliac
Rossini
Rubens
San Gallo
Sansovino
Schiller
Scopas
Sennacherib
St Ambrose
Stephen of Cologne
Theodorus
Thorwaldsen
Tintoretto
Titian
Torell
Torigiano
Velasquez
Vernet
Verrocchio
Vignola
Virgin
Vischer
Weber
William of Sens

LONDON RESIDENTS HONOURED WITH THEIR OWN MUSEUMS

Thomas Carlyle, 24 Cheyne Row, SW3
Sir Winston Churchill, Clive Steps, King Charles Street, SW1
Charles Dickens, 48 Doughty Street, WC1
Michael Faraday, Royal Institution, 21 Albemarle Street, W1
Dr Samuel Johnson, 17 Gough Square, EC4
Sigmund Freud, 20 Maresfield Gardens, NW3
George Frederick Handel, 25 Brook Street W1
William Hogarth, Hogarth's House, Hogarth Lane, W4
John Keats, Wentworth Place, Keats Grove, NW3
Lord Leighton, Leighton House, Holland Park Road, W14
William Morris, Water House, Lloyd Park, E17
Florence Nightingale, Lambeth Palace Road, SE1
Linley Samborne, 18 Stafford Terrace, W8
Sir John Soane, 13 Lincoln's Inn Fields, WC2
The Duke of Wellington, Apsley House, SW1
John Wesley, 47–9 City Road, EC1

VICTORIA CROSS HOLDERS BURIED IN LONDON

Alexander, Ernest Wright (Putney Vale Crematorium)
Bambrick, Valentine (St Pancras & Islington Cemetery, Finchley)
Bent, Spencer John (West Norwood Crematorium)
Boulter, William Ewart (Putney Vale Crematorium)
Buckley, John (Tower Hamlets Cemetery)
Cafe, William Martin (Brompton Cemetery)
Cambridge, Daniel (St Nicholas's Churchyard, Plumstead)
Champion, James (Hammersmith Cemetery)
Collis, James (Wandsworth Cemetery)
Cornwell, John Travers (Manor Park Cemetery)
Crean, Thomas Joseph (St Mary's RC Cemetery, Kensal Rise)
Cross, Arthur Henry (Streatham Vale Cemetery)
Drewry, George Leslie (Manor Park Cemetery)
Durrant, Alfred Edward (Tottenham Cemetery)
Evans, George (Elmers End Cemetery, Beckenham)
Farmer, Joseph John (Brompton Cemetery)
Ffrench, Alfred Kirke (Brompton Cemetery)
Flawn, Thomas (Plumstead Cemetery)
Foster, Edward (Streatham Cemetery)

Fraser, Charles Crauford (Brompton Cemetery)
Freeman, John (Abney Park Cemetery, Stoke Newington)
Grant, Robert (Highgate Cemetery)
Greenwood, Harry (Putney Vale Crematorium)
Hancock, Thomas (Brompton Cemetery)
Harrison, John (Brompton Cemetery)
Hayward, Reginald Frederick Johnson (Putney Vale Crematorium)
Hitch, Frederick (St Nicholas's Churchyard, Old Chiswick)
Home, Sir Anthony Dickson (Highgate Cemetery)
Hope, William (Brompton Cemetery)
Kells, Robert (Lambeth Cemetery)
Ker, Allan Ebenezer (West Hampstead Cemetery)
Kirby, Frank Howard (Streatham Crematorium)
Leitch, Peter (Hammersmith Cemetery)
Lodge, Isaac (Hendon Park Cemetery)
Martin, Cyril Gordon (Eltham Crematorium)
Maude, Frederick Francis (Brompton Cemetery)
Mckenzie, Albert Edward (Camberwell Cemetery)
Monaghan, Thomas (Woolwich Cemetery)
Mullane, Patrick (St Patrick's, Leytonstone)
Nash, William (St John's, Hackney)
O'Connor, Luke (St Mary's RC Cemetery, Kensal Rise)
O'Leary, Michael John (Mill Hill Cemetery)
Parkes, Samuel (Brompton Cemetery)
Percy, Lord Henry Hugh Manvers (St Nicholas Chapel, Westminster
    Abbey)
Reynolds, James Henry (St Mary's RC Cemetery, Kensal Rise)
Richards, Alfred Joseph (Putney Vale Crematorium)
Roberts, Field Marshal Earl (St Paul's Cathedral)
Roberts, James Reynolds (Old Paddington Cemetery)
Ross, John (Islington Cemetery)
Schofield, Harry Norton (Putney Vale Crematorium)
Sims, John Joseph (Manor Park Cemetery)
Smith, Alfred (Plumstead Cemetery)
Spence, David (Lambeth Cemetery)
Stagpoole, Dudley (Hendon Park Cemetery)
Stanlake, William (Camberwell Old Cemetery)
Taylor, John (Woolwich Cemetery)
Wadeson, Richard (Brompton Cemetery)
Walters, George (City of Westminster Cemetery, Finchley)
Warneford, Reginald Alexander John (Brompton Cemetery)
Wheatley, Francis (Brompton Cemetery)

CRIMINALS EXECUTED AND BURIED AT PENTONVILLE

In all 120 men were hanged at Pentonville Gaol between 1902 and 1961, 112 being found guilty of murder, two of treason and six paying the severest penalty for spying during wartime. Among them were the following:

Bush, Edwin Albert Arthur (1961): the last man hanged at Pentonville – on 6 July – for the murder of shop assistant Elsie Batten.

Bywaters, Frederick Edward (1923): murdered his lover's husband. His lover was hanged too, on the same day and at the same time, barely a mile away at Holloway.

Casement, Roger (1916): found guilty of treason during wartime, for which he was also stripped of his knighthood.

Christie, John Reginald (1953): hanged for a number of murders at 10 Rillington Place for which the innocent Timothy John Evans had already been executed.

Crippen, Hawley Harvey (1911): murdered his wife at 39 Hilldrop Crescent and attempted to flee across the Atlantic.

Godhino, Fransisco and Hill, Edward (1911): hanged side-by-side for two unrelated murders.

Heath, Neville George Clevelly (1946): convicted of seriously assaulting and then murdering two women. His plea of insanity was rejected.

Jacoby, Henry Julius (1922): murdered 66-year-old Lady White while robbing her, and was hanged for it while still a teenager.

Macdonald, John (1902): stabbed a man to death in a dispute over 5s.

Meier, Carl (1939–45): was hanged as a spy during the Second World War, together with Jose Waldeburg, Charles Albert Van Der Kieboom, Oswald John Job, Pierre Richard Charles Neukermans and Joseph Jan Van Hove.

Palme-Gotz, Joachim (1939–45): was also hanged during the war, together with Josep Mertins, Heinz Brueling, Erich Koenig and Kurt Zuchlsdorff. Prisoners of war in their early twenties, the five had been convicted of the murder of Sergeant-Major Wolfgang Rosterg. A few weeks later Armin Keuhne and Emil Schmittendorf suffered the same penalty for a similar offence, believing their victim had betrayed their secret escape plans.

Seddon, Frederick Henry (1912): Convicted of poisoning his lodger at 63 Tollington Park, N4, and hanged despite a 250,000-name petition protesting his innocence.

GENERATION X: WHAT LONDON YOUNGSTERS THINK

In 2004 on behalf of the Greater London Authority, hundreds of 11–16-year-olds living in London were questioned in depth about their city.

85%	of young Londoners have never lived anywhere else
82%	think London has a problem with air quality
81%	regard pollution of canals in London as a problem
80%	regard noise pollution in London as a problem
79%	are satisfied with London as a place to live
71%	regard loss of wildlife in London as a problem
60%	say litter in London is a problem
54%	say bullying is a problem where they live
54%	regard graffiti as a problem
52%	think shopping is one of the best things about London
49%	aren't involved with their local community
46%	say there is a problem with bullying on buses
45%	have been a victim of crime
43%	travel to school by public transport
41%	say they would walk or cycle to school if they could
39%	do not think London is a safe place
36%	are concerned about the cost of London living
27%	think the best thing about London is the mix of people
26%	would like cheaper bus and tube fares
22%	have been bullied
7%	do not feel safe at school
6%	rate their school in London as 'very bad'
1%	do not know where their nearest green space is

PERMANENT LONDONERS: THE DEAD ON DISPLAY

With more than 6,500 skeletons in its collection, the Museum of London has recorded the remains from nearly every period in the city's 2,000-year history. Each bone provides researchers and visitors with a unique insight into the lives of Londoners past and present.

Prehistoric: Shepperton Woman, *c.* 3600 BC. The oldest known remains found in the London area, her skeleton shows she had good teeth but a bad back.

Early English: Harper Road, Southwark: Perhaps our first real Londoner, dating back to AD 50, she was 5ft 2in and buried in a simple wooden coffin together with personal effects including pottery, a bronze mirror and some simple jewellery.

Roman: A female buried at Aldgate suggests most Roman Londoners enjoyed adequate nutrition although tuberculosis (an indicator of crowded living conditions and poor hygiene) was a problem. A mere 10.5% survived beyond age 45, but surprisingly only 15.5% of those buried at the site were under 18.

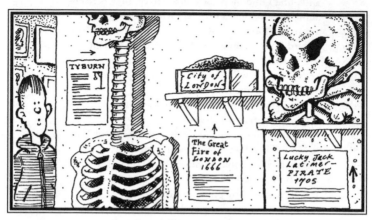

Saxon: London's population having collapsed after the Romans left, Saxon Londoners were rare and their remains even more so. A female found near Fenchurch Street station, however, had poor teeth indicating honey and ale in the diet while other graves contain tweezers, picks, even cosmetic brushes, suggesting an interest in personal appearance.

Norman: Bodies found beneath St Nicholas Shambles on Newgate Street indicate a poor diet and evidence of a hard life. Most were still dying before the age of 45, and many showed signs of poverty and foot problems resulting from poorly fitting shoes.

Medieval: A plentiful supply of bodies from St John's Clerkenwell and plague pits such the one at East Smithfield indicate a thriving city but dire poverty for many inhabitants. With essentials in London costing 50% more than elsewhere in the country, malnutrition was commonplace along with chronic amaemia and growth disorders showing up in the teeth and bones.

Georgian/Victorian: Measurements of skeletons found at Christ Church, Spitalfields, are shorter on average than their medieval forebears, their growth patterns perhaps compromised by food supply as well as the 'smoak' and pollution. The lack of sunlight (a vital source of Vitamin D) would have fostered the incidence of rickets.

5

TRANSPORT FOR LONDON

SOME UNEXPECTED LONDON TRANSPORT FIRSTS

One of those many things which Londoners take for granted, a handy but unremarkable refuge for pedestrians, the first ever traffic island was the invention of a Colonel Pierpoint who came up with the idea in 1864. Placing his prototype just south of Piccadilly in St James's Street, in order that he could cross safely to his club, he was understandably proud of his creation but one day turned round to admire it, missed his footing and was promptly run over by a cab.

The first ever multi-storey car park made a surprisingly early debut too, opening for business in 1901 when cars were still quite a rarity. Located immediately behind Piccadilly Circus in Denman Street (where today NCP offers a similar service) the City & Suburban Electric Carriage Company offered 19,000sq. ft spread over no fewer than seven storeys with the upper ones being reached via a hydraulic lift capable of raising a 3-ton vehicle.

London's first set of traffic lights was similarly ill-fated. Gas-powered and installed in Parliament Square in 1868, it blew up killing a policeman and causing the mounts of a passing platoon of cavalry to stampede. The first electric set was erected in Piccadilly Circus on 3 August 1926.

Clearly, more than a century ago, parking in central London was already quite a problem – which begs the question: why did it take so long to introduce the parking meter? In fact it wasn't until 1958 that the first of these arrived, a small number being installed on the streets of Mayfair with a charge of 1s being sufficient to keep the authorities at bay for a full hour. Today the same fee buys you 45 seconds.

London can also lay claim to Britain's first fully functioning self-service petrol station which opened for business at the southern end of Southwark Bridge in November 1961. An experimental one had been installed at Patcham in Sussex, but the slot meter proved too easy for the locals to fiddle.

Today London's oldest petrol station is the Village Garage in Bloomsbury, which opened in 1926, having been built for the Duke of Bedford on his London estate.

The deepest car park in London is on the same estate, buried beneath Bloomsbury Square. An exercise in 1960s engineering excess it descends through 60ft and seven storeys, has room for an incredible 450 private cars, but ruined the Repton landscape up above.

LETTING THE TRAIN TAKE THE STRAIN

Today there are approximately 940 railway stations in the London area, including 255 on the London Underground and a further thirty-eight as part of the Docklands Light Railway or DLR.

Having overtaken Liverpool Street, the busiest station with 77.5 million passengers a year is now King's Cross St Pancras, but Waterloo traditionally has the biggest morning rush-hour peak.

Of the one million commuters who travel to London each weekday morning between 7am and 10am, approximately three-quarters arrive by tube or train.

Having risen by well over a quarter since 1995, passenger volumes on the tube now amount to just under 980 million passenger journeys per year, with an additional 50 million passenger journeys a year on the DLR.

This compares to about 1.6 billion trips made by London buses over the same period, the statistics reflecting the fact that even now an estimated 40 per cent of London households do not yet own a car.

Tunnelling in London pre-dates the tube by many years – preparatory work on the first Thames Tunnel started in 1805 – but it received its first real boost when engineer Marc Brunel invented his revolutionary tunnelling machine. This he did after studying the activities of the common shipworm *Teredo navalis* while serving time in a debtors' prison when the defeat of Napoleon caused his businesses to collapse.

Brunel took over the tunnel project in 1825, but progress was so slow that when it finally opened on 25 March 1843 what had started out as an exciting exercise in national pride had been nicknamed 'the Great Bore' by *The Times*. Even then it was suitable only for pedestrian traffic, and wasn't finally incorporated into the railway network until December 1869 when it became the world's first underwater train tunnel.

The word 'tube' was first coined for the railway in 1890, when the first deep level electric line was commissioned. The network wasn't officially branded the 'Underground' for another seventeen years.

The tube network covers more than 630 square miles and in fact a mere 45 per cent of the routes actually run underground. Most of those which do still follow the route of major streets and rarely pass under buildings because many Londoners at the time feared the tunnels would undermine building foundations or simply collapse.

The world's longest continuous railway tunnel is still the Northern Line, which runs from East Finchley to Morden via Bank. With twenty-four stations and three junctions, it runs for a total of 17 miles and 528 yards.

When a new stretch of the Piccadilly Line tunnel was excavated from Finsbury Park to Hammersmith in July 1902, the spoil was used to build up the terraces at Chelsea's Stamford Bridge football ground.

Sheltering from the Blitz, on the night of 27 September 1940 an incredible 117,000 slept in the Underground.

With the tube network now comprising 253 miles of railway lines and 112 lifts, the deepest station on the network is Hampstead at 192ft below street level. From there the tunnels go deeper still, the Northern Line reaching its lowest point 221ft below Holly Bush Hill.

By contrast the highest station is Amersham on the Metropolitan Line. Well clear of London itself, this is around 490ft above sea level. The highest elevation any line achieves above ground level, however, is a mere 60ft at the Dollis Hill Viaduct.

Since the lovley little Ongar branch closed in 1994 the longest journey one can make on the tube without changing trains is the 34.1 miles from Epping to West Ruislip. The longest gap between stations is 3.89 miles from Chesham to Chalfont & Latimer, and the shortest a mere quarter of a mile from Covent Garden to Leicester Square.

In central London the need to slow down for stations means trains rarely travel at more than 30mph; because of this the Metropolitan is the fastest line, with trains on the way out to Amersham recording up to 60mph, with the average speed across the network being closer to 20mph.

The Busiest Lines	Passengers per year	Number of stations on the line
Northern	207,000,000	50
Central	184,000,000	49
Piccadilly	176,000,000	52
District	173,000,000	60
Victoria	161,000,000	16
Jubilee	128,000,000	27
Bakerloo	96,000,000	25
Circle	68,000,000	27
Metropolitan	54,000,000	34
Hammersmith & City	46,000,000	28
East London	10,000,000	8
Waterloo & City	10,000,000	2

Next time you find one of the escalators at your local station still not working, you may like to reflect on the fact that maintenance staff are responsible for 412 of them. Waterloo alone has 25 (plus two conveyors) but the longest at 197ft is at Angel while Chancery Lane has the shortest, at just 30ft.

A survey in 2004 determined that the most popular song performed by buskers on the London Underground was 'Wonderwall' by Oasis.

To power the network the gas turbine power station at Greenwich uses an incredible 5,400 tons of natural gas a year, producing 1,091 gigawatt hours of power, enabling the rails to carry a nominal charge of 630 volts (DC). At the same time hundreds of pumps on the network discharge approximately 30 million litres of water per day, at a rate sufficient to fill a normal municipal swimming pool every 20 minutes.

GHOST STATIONS ON THE NETWORK

The London rail system has an incredible forty or so abandoned, disused or so-called 'ghost' stations, many of which can be still be seen at street level. Some closed shortly after opening, at least one before a single passenger had even been through the turnstiles. Many others have been left behind as lines have shifted, or new stations have been opened nearby using the same or a similar name.

Among the more interesting are:

Aldwych (1907–94): No trains pass so it cannot be seen. However the station still exists and is frequently used for filming and can even be hired for parties. Built on the site of the Royal Strand Theatre, the ghost of a dead actress is reported to haunt its platforms.

British Museum (1908–33): This can be glimpsed through the window as you travel between Tottenham Court Road and Holborn on the Central Line. Effectively replaced by the new Holborn station in 1933, it was used by the Ministry of Defence during the Second World War and is still held by the Brigade of Guards.

Brompton Road (1906–34): Another Piccadilly Line station, situated between Knightsbridge and South Kensington stations, the platforms were bricked up and converted into offices. The deep liftshaft became an operations centre for anti-aircraft guns in the 1940s.

Down Street (1907–32): The claret tilework can still be seen at street level, and brickwork on the tunnel wall changes colour as you travel between Green Park and Hyde Park Corner. Briefly Churchill's wartime HQ, the PM's personal bath is rumoured still to be *in situ*.

King William Street (1890–1900): Close to the Monument, this station was used as an air raid shelter for up to 100,000 people at a time – some wartime posters still survive on the walls – and now carries fibre-optic and other communications cables under the river.

Mark Lane (1884–1967): Closed on 4 February 1967 when the new Tower Hill station opened in its place. It can be seen when travelling between Monument and Tower Hill on the District Line.

North End (1907): Better known as Bull & Bush, the station can clearly be seen between Hampstead and Golders Green on the Northern Line. Uniquely it was mothballed before a single passenger had used it.

South Kentish Town (1907–24): Between Kentish Town and Camden Town on the Northern Line it closed during a strike in June 1924 and never reopened. It was recently converted into a sauna and massage parlour.

St Mary's (1884–1938): Between Aldgate East and Whitechapel on the District Line, it proved too close to both and too small to be useful.

Stockwell (1890–1923): Originally the southern terminal of the City and South London Line, now the Northern Line and as such the city's oldest deep-level railway, the station was closed on 28 November 1923, but reopened in December 1924 slightly further south. The original station can still be seen from passing trains.

Tower of London (1882–4): On the same site as Tower Hill station, this one closed after just two years when the nearby and much larger Mark Lane station opened.

Wood Lane (1908–47): Many years ago the last station on the Central Line before it pushed out to the western suburbs, its platforms and stairs can be seen from eastbound trains as you leave White City and enter the first underground tunnel.

York Road (1906–32): This can be seen from both directions while travelling on the Piccadilly Line but for the best view, look out of the right-hand window travelling from Caledonian Road to King's Cross.

INCREDIBLE STUFF HANDED IN TO LOST PROPERTY

One lawnmower

Several silicon breast implants

A bishop's crook

An outboard motor from a boat

An entire garden bench

A sealed box containing three dead bats

An artificial leg

Several glass eyes

One stuffed gorilla

A wheelchair

Two human skulls in a bag

LOOPY SCHEMES WHICH MUST HAVE SEEMED A GOOD IDEA AT THE TIME

London's first ever railway, the London & Greenwich Line, ran almost its entire 3.75-mile length along an elevated viaduct. The trains thus avoided the usual congestion at ground level, but doing it this way required the expensive and time-consuming construction of no fewer than 878 brick arches.

Another early venture, the 1840 Blackwall Railway from Blackwall to the Minories, used stationary engines at either end instead of locomotives. These slowly hauled the carriages along using stout cables fitted to the carriage-ends.

'Fowler's Ghost' was the nickname given to a pioneering 1861 design by London engineer Sir John Fowler. A smokeless engine designed for London's new underground network, it was fuelled by red-hot bricks placed under the boiler but made only one brief experimental run.

Instead, and because ejecting smoke into London's new underground tunnels clearly wasn't a sensible option, the smoke on early Metropolitan Line trains was initially routed into tanks fitted to the locomotives which could be discharged each time a train broke cover.

Another alternative was tried in 1864 at Crystal Palace. Here a new type of 'atmospheric railway' worked by tightly fitting the carriages into a circular tunnel like a piston and forcing them along using only air pressure.

Yet another plan to come a cropper was Professor Sir Patrick Abercrombie's in 1943 calling for tunnels to be excavated all over the place in order to reduce congestion on the surface. Unfortunately he proposed running a really big one right under Buckingham Palace, a major tactical error on his part as he sorrowfully admitted after the plans had been shelved.

Then, as recently as 1967, and clearly with no regard whatsoever for the architectural environment, the Greater London Council commissioned a feasibility study for twin overhead passenger monorails to run down the middle of Nash's Regent Street.

THE MACHINE THAT CHANGED THE WORLD (AND LONDON)

It's hard to believe now, but cars weren't always popular. In the early days the *Times* thundered against the exploits of what it termed 'these motorious carbarians'. *Punch* carried a cartoon featuring a hapless driver called Mr Newfangle. And the Marquess of Queensberry sought permission with a private Act of Parliament to shoot pioneering automobilists whom he thought presented a danger to himself and his family.

Other opponents of progress called for cars to be fitted with explosive devices which would detonate if the driver exceeded a certain (suspiciously low) speed. And even Henry Ford admitted that had he asked the public what they wanted they'd have told him 'just build me a faster horse'.

But clearly no-one could uninvent the motor car and return to the horse, and at least the typhoid rates in London dropped off once the wheel replaced the hoof and great piles of dung began to disappear from the streets.

That said, the fatalities on London's roads leapt from 5 to 291 from 1901–11 as the motor car moved from being an elitist plaything to genuine mass transport. This transformation was largely as the result of a drop in new car prices, from an average of £684 in 1920 to just £279 eight years later. Little wonder sales rocketed sixteen-fold in less than 20 years.

In 1938, and starting at the foot of the M1 in north London, official surveyors sketched out the first 1,000 miles of British motorways – doing so in crayon on a map given away free with *Tit-Bits* magazine.

In London itself, however, average speeds in the capital quickly dropped back to pre-1908 levels, a consequence not just of greater congestion but also a lack of parking restrictions and a chaotic combination on the capital's roads of cars and cabs, trucks, buses and horse-drawn wagons. Since when, of course, there's been little or no improvement.

Indeed by 1928 London's Director of Roads had declared the worst blackspot to be Hyde Park Corner 'through which more traffic passes in 24 hours than any other other place in the world'. By 1998 this had been supplanted by Vauxhall Cross which, with an estimated 1,500,000 cars by now running round London on a typical weekday, is reckoned to be the busiest road junction in the whole of Europe.

CARS WITH CAPITAL CONNECTIONS

The only make of car to derive its moniker from London is the Vauxhall, named after its erstwhile riverside home in Lambeth. The original factory took its name from the home of a Norman knight who once lived on the same spot, Fulk Le Bréant of Fulk's or Fawke's Hall. When the company relocated to Luton in Bedfordshire, coincidentally where the same warrior had his country seat, it took his heraldic emblem to use as the company logo.

In those early days Vauxhall was far from alone in London. Walter Owen Bentley first set up shop in Cricklewood, Messrs Bamford & Martin did likewise in Kensington before renaming the firm Aston Martin and moving to Feltham, and after studying engineering at University College Colin Chapman of Lotus built a prototype at Wood Green, afterwards moving his fledgling operation to Hornsey where he stayed until 1959.

Rather more mysterious were the goings-on at E.H. Owen, another Kensington-based car maker. A somewhat shadowy outfit it advertised its vehicles in the *Autocar* and elsewhere from 1899 until 1935, often at prices higher than Rolls-Royce's. The truth, however, is that no such car as an 'Owen' was ever seen, nor has the precise location of the factory ever quite been located. The company address was listed as 72 Comeragh Road, renumbered no. 6 after the war, but the premises here were clearly not suitable for actual manufacture.

Willesden though was certainly home to the Legros & Knowles factory, and from 1905 until the outbreak of the First World War it churned out a succession of cumbersome and rather crudely-made tourers named Iris after the Classical goddess. She of course was known as the Speedy Messenger of the Gods, which didn't sound like this car at all, although the name was also said by the factory to indicate (no less optimistically) that 'It Runs in Silence'.

In 1952 the first Reliant Regal was actually banned from appearing at the London Motor Show because the organisers were of the opinion that the diminutive three-wheeler couldn't honestly be classified it as a car.

Similarly when Giovanni Michelotti's new Triumph Herald was unveiled in 1959, an MP tabled a question in the House asking whether it was really necessary for British car makers to resort to using designers 'from the land of spaghetti'.

TOFFS ON WHEELS

No shrinking violet, Lord Kitchener had his Rolls-Royce painted bright yellow in order that he would be instantly recognised when driving around London.

In July 1922, accompanied by his dog, the Duke of Leinster set off from London in his Rolls-Royce reaching Aberdeen in just 14 hours to win a massive £3,000 wager with a friend.

When he was President of the Royal Automobile Club in Pall Mall, the old Duke of Sutherland used to keep the engine of one of his four Rolls-Royces running constantly in order that it would be ready should he wish to make an immediate departure.

Meanwhile as president of the rival Automobile Association the 5th Earl of Lonsdale ordered his domestic servants into yellow livery to match the organisation's own colours and told his gardeners to repaint all their wheelbarrows a similar hue.

Charles Chetwynd-Talbot, the 23rd Lord Shrewsbury, is the only earl to have a make of motor car named after him. The cars were manufactured in Ladbroke Grove.

After colliding with another car in 1961 Lord Derby (whose London home is now the Oriental Club in Stratford Place, W1) successfully escaped prosecution by claiming his view had been restricted by the long bonnet of his Rolls-Royce.

Earl Russell, the philosopher Bertrand Russell's brother and a fierce defender of early motorists' rights, queued all night to obtain the first ever car registration plate (A1). He later served time for bigamy, however, with even his parents admitting he was 'a limb of satan'.

Resident in Berkeley Square, the Rt Hon. John Theodore Cuthbert Moore-Brabazon, later Lord Brabazon of Tara, owned the first car in the country with metallic paint. A pale blue Aston Martin which now resides in Suffolk, the unusual paint effect was said to have been disovered by accident when the ball bearings in a paint-grinding machine broke up.

Mayfair-based Lord Howe took up motor racing between the wars at the suggestion of a magistrate who was fed up with fining him for speeding. Subsequently his speed in a 1.5 litre Delage around the outer circuit at Brooklands was never surpassed, and driving with Capt. Sir Henry 'Tim' Birkin Bt he won at Le Mans in an Alfa Romeo.

OTHER NOTABLE LONDON MOTORISTS

Living in Chelsea's Cheyne Walk, Rolling Stones guitarist Keith Richard at one point had his Bentley S3 Flying Spur fitted with Turkish flags in order to fool the police that he had diplomatic immunity.

In 1952 south London garage owner Sydney Allard became the first and so far only man to win the Monte Carlo Rally in a car of his own design.

Another London car dealer with an impressive track record was three-times Formula One World Champion Sir Jack Brabham, who had a showroom selling Malaysian-built Proton.

After racing driver Percy Lambert was killed in an accident at Brooklands in 1913 he was buried at Brompton Cemetery in a streamlined coffin designed to match his car.

Born in north London, Rod Stewart claims he quit The Faces in order to go solo so that he could earn the £1,000 he needed to buy a Marcos sports car.

In the late 1950s the British Motor Corporation boss Sir Leonard Lord encouraged the launch of the bestselling Mini in order to get 'these bloody awful bubble cars off the streets of London'.

THE WORLD'S FAVOURITE AIRPORT?

Heathrow Airport takes its name from a little hamlet long since obliterated (together with Perry Oaks and Kings Arbour) to make room for Terminal 3. The first airfield was conceived initially as a military aerodrome, and work on this near to the modest, experimental Great West Aerodrome of 1929 began on the site in the early 1940s.

However, by the time the contractors had completed the task the war was over and the site was transferred to the civilian sector. The first commercial flight was made on New Year's Day 1946 by a British South American Airways Lancastrian bound for Buenos Aires. This was a civilianised but still fantastically uncivilised version of the wartime Lancaster bomber, the customs and immigration officials still at this time being housed in Army surplus tents.

In the 1950s an early prototype of Jaguar's C-Type sports car was tested on the main runway at Heathrow where it reached 120mph. Today, with 470,000 take-offs and landings a year, such a feat would probably be discouraged.

Operating 24 hours a day, 365 days a year, Heathrow despatches 67.7 million passengers a year courtesy of approximately 90 airlines. Only 1% of flights from Heathrow involve non-jet aircraft. It is also the country's largest port, accounting for more trade than any sea port in the UK.

Scheduled flights from Heathrow leave for 186 different destinations. According to the airport's operator BAA, Heathrow's top ten international destinations are:

1. New York
2. Dublin
3. Paris
4. Amsterdam
5. Frankfurt
6. Los Angeles
7. Hong Kong
8. Dubai
9. Madrid
10. Toronto

Heathrow's top domestic destinations are Edinburgh, Glasgow, Manchester, Belfast and Aberdeen.

In addition to four terminals (with a fifth currently under construction) the airport has two runways, the longest of which is 3,902 metres long and 45 metres wide, also 531 check-in desks and 264 aircraft stands. The terminals also accommodate an estimated 48,000sq m of retail space, while of the airport's 34,603 parking spaces just under half are reserved for airport staff leaving another 50,000 airport workers to make alternative travel arrangements.

In a survey in 2006 of more than sixty possible venues on the leading budget travel website www.sleepinginairports.com, Heathrow Airport emerged as the most popular place in Europe in which to bunk down for nothing.

In this and in terms of overall passenger numbers still the world's most popular airport, Heathrow nevertheless attracts thousands of letters of complaints each year of which approximately 15% relate to catering and 12% to lost or damaged baggage.

SOME TAXI FACTS

Licensed cabs – the name derives from the French, *cabriolet de place* – have a surprisingly ancient heritage, the now defunct Corporation of Coachmen having first secured a charter to ply for hire in London in 1639.

Despite licensing they failed to attract the right sort of passenger, however, so that in 1694 a bevy of females in one cab reportedly behaved so badly in the environs of Hyde Park that the authorities responded by banning hired cabs from the park for the next 230 years.

By mid-Victorian times the drivers too had acquired a bit of a reputation, prompting a number of philanthropists to pay for the erection of London's distinctive green cab shelters. Places where drivers could eat rather than drink alcohol, and where discussion of politics was strictly forbidden, sixty-four were built although only around a dozen still remain.

The term Hackney Carriage has no connection with the east London suburb but rather comes from the old French *haquenée*, meaning an ambling nag.

London's first mechanically driven taxis made their debut in December 1897 but were at this point battery- rather than petrol-powered. The novelty value of the quiet-running vehicles operated by the London Electric Cab Company was high, but unfortunately the considerable weight of batteries carried on board meant that they were actually even slower than the horse-drawn competition.

As a result, having led the world with this new technology in the closing days of the Victorian era, by the turn of the century the company was bankrupt and five years later there were a mere 19 electric cabs still up and running. This compares to 10,361 of the conventional horse-drawn variety, at least one of which – a four-wheeled 'growler' – remained in service at Victoria station until 1947.

Despite Gottlieb Daimler having invented the internal combustion engine in 1883 – and built the first petrol-powered cab just four years later – the Metropolitan Police was slow to move and refused to license such a device until 1904. Two years later they instigated a series of new regulations – including the requirement for a tight 25ft turning circle – some of which are still in force a century later.

The taximeter was invented in 1891 by another German, Wilhelm Bruhn, and gives the cab its other familiar name. It was introduced in London in 1907, indicating the distance travelled to the passenger in order to prevent rows with the driver about the final fare.

Although the new petrol-powered taxis quickly proved popular with punter and driver alike, their numbers slumped by almost 60% during the First World War when widespread oil shortages gave their horse-drawn rivals something of a renaissance. The advent of the more economical diesel cab in 1966 finally rescued the mechanically driven cab, however, and by 1996 when London had 22,000 licensed drivers and 17,000 licensed cabs all but seventeen were diesel.

When a special Buckingham Palace Brownie Pack was formed for Princess Anne in 1959, one of the other nine-year-olds handpicked to keep her company was the daughter of a London cabbie.

The classic London black cab is the Austin FX-4. It was introduced in 1958 and remained in production until 1996, a record for a British vehicle and unrivalled except by the Mini. In 1989 a version of the FX-4 went on sale in Japan badged as the 'Big Ben Novelty Car'.

In the 1960s the fabulously wealthy oil heir Nubar Gulbenkian had a uniquely luxurious limousine built on an FX-4 taxi chassis for use when he was in London. 'Apparently it can turn on a sixpence', he used to tell acquaintances, 'whatever that is.'

6

BUSINESS & LEISURE

BUSINESS: THE BANK OF ENGLAND

The idea of a Bank of England was actually a Scottish invention. William Paterson thought it up as a security measure after the various borrowings of the Stuart kings from the Royal Mint threatened to destabilise the country, but unfortunately one of the bank's first directors embezzled £29,000. This was never recovered.

The Bank issued its first notes in 1725, including a £100 note at the time when a mere £20 would reportedly have secured an entire house, fully furnished, in Pall Mall for a year.

The nickname, 'the Old Lady of Threadneedle Street', was coined by the playwright Richard Sheridan in a speech to the House of Commons in 1797. James Gillray then used it in a cartoon, and the name has stuck.

In 1836 a sewer worker successfully penetrated the Bank's bullion room and was given a substantial reward for his honesty after sending an anonymous note to bank officials arranging to meet them 'at a dark and midnight hour'. Having stumbled upon an easy route into the gold store from Dowgate, he showed them how he had done it enabling the Bank to quickly seal the breach.

In 1780, during the anti-Catholic Gordon Riots, volunteers from the Bank aided by members of the militia repelled the rioters using bullets made by melting down their inkwells. Thereafter the Bank was protected each night by an armed military detachment called the Bank Guard or Picquet, an arrangement which was finally cancelled only in 1973.

During rebuilding work in 1933 a lead coffin was found under the Bank containing the body of former clerk William Jenkins. Being more than 6ft 7in tall, he so feared being stolen by bodysnatchers – they had already attempted to buy him in advance for 200 guineas knowing they could sell his corpse to unscrupulous surgeons – that after his death his friends asked and obtained permission for him to be buried in the Bank's Garden Court.

OTHER BANKING FACTS

We take it for granted now but although the facsimile signature of the Chief Cashier has been a feature of British banknotes since 1870 the monarch's portrait did not appear on any of them until 1960.

The father of British banking was the Lord Mayor of London Sir Francis Child (1642–1713). Inheriting a goldsmith's business founded as long ago as 1559, he transformed it into a bank. Child & Company then opened for business in 1673 'at the Marygold by Temple Bar' before moving to no. 1 Fleet Street.

With a value of £10 the earliest known cheque was drawn on bankers Clayton & Morris of Cornhill on 22 April 1659. It was auctioned at Sotheby's three centuries later and fetched 130 times its face value.

The first cashpoint machine was installed at Barclays Bank in Church Street, Enfield, in June 1967, but in an age before plastic it required customers to use paper vouchers encoded with punch-holes. Together with a personal ID number punched into the machine via a computer keyboard these authorised the machine to dispense £10 notes but unfortunately the somewhat over-complex contraption was notoriously prone to technical problems.

C. Hoare & Co. is Britain's oldest privately owned bank. Established in 1672, the bank today is an eleventh-generation family firm run by no fewer than nine direct descendants of the founder. The front door can be locked only from the inside, because day and night at least one of them is always on the premises should any of its 10,000 customers call.

London's first drive-in bank, designed with passing motorists in mind, was installed by the venerable Drummond's Bank, a branch of the Royal Bank of Scotland housed in a building by Admiralty Arch on Trafalgar Square.

Although for many years now a part of the National Westminster Banking group, Coutts & Co. is by far the most famous of the 'posh' banks – perhaps because it has handled the accounts of every British monarch since George III.

The first time anyone in the City used the term 'Black Friday' was way back in 1866 when the private banking house of Overend, Gurney & Company collapsed, causing everyone else to panic.

ENDURING APPEAL:
SEVEN OF THE OLDEST SHOPS IN TOWN

James Lock & Co., St James's Street, SW1
In 1676 Lock inherited his father-in-law's hatter's business, moved here shortly afterwards and it is still family run. Nelson called in immediately before departing for Trafalgar to pay a bill for a hat with a special built-in eye-shade, and Wellington wore one of its plumed hats at Waterloo. Lock also sold the first ever bowler hat, but shop staff insist they are called 'cokes' after the Norfolk man who ordered several for his gamekeepers.

J. Floris, Jermyn Street, SW1

Juan Famenisas Floris, a Spaniard from Minorca, first set up shop here as a barber and perfumer in 1730, the company receiving its first royal warrant in 1821. The beautiful display cases which line the walls are the originals, dating back to the Great Exhibition in 1851.

Twining & Co., Strand, WC2

Richard Twining set up shop here in 1707 as a tea and coffee seller to Queen Anne making this the oldest rate-payer on the books at the City of Westminster, and almost certainly the oldest business in the UK still carrying on its original trade on its original site.

Fortnum & Mason, Piccadilly, SW1

In 1707 a footman to Queen Anne charged with replenishing the royal candelabra, William Fortnum amassed a modest sum selling the part-used candles to the Queen's ladies. Handing in his cards at St James's Palace, he went into into partnership with a friend Hugh Mason selling 'hart's horn, gableworm seed, saffron and dirty white candy'. Among the first to sell Heinz's new canned goods, for years the store also had a separate department dealing with supplies of pies, preserves and puddings to the neighbouring gentlemen's clubs of St James's. The figures on the clock outside come out to the strains of the 'Eton Boating Song'.

Berry Brothers & Rudd, St James's Street, SW1

An eighth-generation family firm, 'established in the XVIIth century' as the sign outside declares, distinguished customers of London's oldest wine merchants have included Lord Byron, the dandy Beau Brummell, George IV, and even King Louis-Philippe of France and Napoleon III.

Henry Poole & Co, Cork Street, W1

James Poole stitched his own tunic for the Volunteer Corps, received many requests for something similar and by 1822 had opened for business as a specialist military tailor. With the back door on to Savile Row soon becoming the main entrance to his premises, the company was thus the first of many tailors to make Savile Row what it is today.

Messrs. Paxton & Whitfield, Jermyn Street, SW1
The celebrated Suffolk cheesemonger and provisions merchant moved to its present premises in 1797. For almost sixty years before this, however, the same business had been active at Clare Market, established on land owned by the Earl of Clare and on which the London School of Economics now stands.

STUFF ABOUT SHOPPING EVERYONE OUGHT TO KNOW

The Japanese term for a business suit is a *sebiro*, a simple transliteration of 'Savile Row'.

A legal technicality called *market ouvert* meant that for years, 806 of them in fact, anything bought between sunrise and sunset from a stallholder at New Caledonian Market became the legal property of the buyer even if it subsequently turned out to be stolen. Now better known as Bermondsey Antiques Market, the stallholders finally relinquished this arcane right when the twelfth-century law was repealed in 1995.

J.C. Cording of Piccadilly, long established as suppliers of traditional tweeds, classic covert coats and cords to the huntin', shootin' and fishin' set is part-owned by ageing rocker Eric Clapton.

Although neon lights weren't to become a feature of London until the 1930s, Piccadilly Circus was already blazing with electrically illuminated advertising as early as 1893.

Gordon Selfridge installed a secret lift in the store so his girlfriends could arrive unobserved, while at Whiteley's the proprietor was actually murdered by an illegitimate son whom he wished to disown.

The 1970s sitcom *Are You Being Served?* was in large part based on its writer's experience of working as an assistant at Simpsons on Piccadilly.

With the iconic tube map more or less centred on Oxford Circus, shoppers using the four underground stations on Oxford Street itself account for more than 100,000,000 passenger journeys annually.

Old Bond Street is actually barely fourteen years older than New Bond Street, and both acquired the aristocratic seal of approval only after the influential Duchess of Devonshire in 1784 organised a boycott of the hitherto smarter shops of Covent Garden.

Among the bizarre stuff ordered from the store by Harrods customers are a skunk intended for the buyer's ex-wife and a fossil found in Texas, imported to the UK, bought by a Texan on a trip to London and then exported back to the USA.

LONDON'S ODDEST JOBS

The Ravenmaster at the Tower of London is charged with ensuring that the ravens don't leave the tower, as tradition dictates the Crown will fall if they do. An important role it is nevertheless a relatively easy task as the birds all have their wings clipped to prevent them flying away.

His boss, the Constable of the Tower, has for over 600 years been officially authorised to extract a barrel of rum from any naval vessel using the river. He is also entitled to any livestock which falls off London Bridge, a penny for each leg of any animal which falls into the moat, and tuppence from any pilgrims arriving to visit the shrine of St James.

The Master Reader of the Honourable Society of the Middle Temple is the chap who, when lawyers are called to the Bar, actually calls them. This he does by way of inviting them to sign their names in a book on 'the Cupboard', the name given to the table upon which empty cups are placed after mealtimes.

In the church of St Margaret Pattens, Rood Lane, EC3, is a seventeenth-century memorial to James Donalson who was the 'City Garbler', a person who specialised in selecting spices.

Fluffers, though now largely replaced by machines, were employed on the Underground for years, walking the tunnels each night to collect and remove waste material left behind by the passengers. The largest single component of this waste is human hair – a lovely thought.

Lady herb-strewers were traditionally employed to scatter sweet-smelling petals wherever the monarch processed – within the royal apartments, as well as outside on the streets – and today the Fellowes family still claim the hereditary right on behalf of their eldest unmarried daughter.

The Doyen of the Court of St James's is the longest-serving diplomat who by virtue of this takes precedence over all the other diplomats in the Court. The position is held regardless of any treaties or the relative status or strategic importance of the other diplomats' home countries, the term itself comes from the old French for Dean.

The Queen's Remembrancer, invariably a senior judge, is responsible for collecting so-called 'quit rents' such as the pair of knives – one sharp, one blunt – payable in London each year for a small scrap of land in Shropshire, and the six horseshoes which comprise the rent for a tenement (now long gone) near St Clement Danes.

In London the 'heyday of the whore' was in the 1860s when an estimated 80,000 prostitutes touted for business in a city only a third the size of London today. Numbers had declined a hundred years later but during the Profumo Affair Harold Wilson was still heard complaining about 'a system of society which pays a harlot 25 times as much as it pays its prime minister'.

FOURTEEN FORGOTTEN LONDON FIRSTS

Escalator: Not an enthusiast of the new-fangled 'ascending rooms' or lifts which were sweeping the capital, in 1898 the manager of Harrods ordered an escalator instead. Such was the experience of travelling on it that he was forced to engage the services of an attendant dispensing brandy to gentlemen shoppers and Epsom Salts to the ladies.

Fax: the first commercial picture ever sent by fax was a newspaper photograph sent from London to Paris in 1907.

Anti-Smoking Campaign: As early as 1601 a London pamphleteer was railing against the harmful effects of 'this filthie custome'. Then in 1604 James I published a rant of his own, arguing that the habit

was 'lothsome to the eye, hatefull to the Nose, harmfull to the brain, dangerous to the Lungs'.

Baseball: The Americans play it best, but the earliest known reference to the game of 'base-ball' appeared in London in 1844 in *The Little Pretty Pocket Book*, a popular volume which was not published in the Americas for another 43 years.

Dirigible: The first powered flight by an airship was made using propellers driven by clockwork to power a scale model created by Monck Mason in 1843.

Gas Lighting: The Chinese ran gas through bamboo pipes as early as 500 BC, but London didn't follow suit until 1805 when the splendidly named New Patriotic Imperial and National Light and Heat Company equipped Pall Mall to become the first street in the country to be lit by gas.

Hydrogen: 'Inflammable air' was first discovered in 1766 by Henry Cavendish at his private laboratory in central London. Fifteen years later he was able to manufacture water by exploding his new gas in the presence of oxygen.

Jigsaw: The world's first jigsaw was created by London engraver John Spilsbury. Keen that children should make their own entertainment, in 1761 he created what he called 'disected maps' pasting them on to boards and cutting them out by hand.

Ice-Skating: London built the world's first ice-rink, the Glacarium, in 1873 which was decorated with murals showing delightful Alpine scenes. It first became an Olympic sport at the London games in 1908.

Plastic: The world's first plastic, Parkesine, was created by Alexander Parkes in 1845 using a base of nitro-cellulose. Producing a range of billiard balls, combs, pens and decorative plaques, the new material made its debut at the International Exhibition in London, but his venture failed because the products tended to explode.

Plate-glass Window: In 1801 men's outfitter Francis Place spent a fortune on a large window for his shop at 16 Charing Cross Road, but maintained he was more than remunerated when business picked up as a consequence of his lavish window displays.

Roller Skates: first worn at a masque at Carlisle House, Soho Square, the inventor Joseph Merlin unfortunately came a cropper after attempting to play the violin while rolling into the ballroom at speed. Crashing into a large mirror, he was seriously injured.

Steel-framed Store: The elegant premises of the outfitters Simpsons in Piccadilly (now a branch of Waterstones) was the country's first steel-framed shop.

Video Recording Machinery: This was on sale at Major Radiovision of Wigmore Street, W1, in June 1935. Using discs rather than tapes, each could hold 12 minutes of images with sound and cost 7s.

Blue Plaques Commemorating Things, not People

The first official London plaque was installed in 1867 by the Royal Society of Arts. By 1901 its officers had erected thirty-six plaques, the oldest surviving ones being in honour of Napoleon III and John Dryden (both 1875). The responsibility passed to the London County Council in 1901, then the GLC and now lies with English Heritage. Approximately twelve are authorised each year, but it is sometimes overlooked that of the approximately 700 now in place not all commemorate individuals.

Television: World's first regular broadcast service from Alexandra Palace, N22, on 2 November 1936.

Cato Street Conspiracy: Discovered at 1a Cato Street, W1, on 23 February 1820.

Chelsea China: First manufactured in Lawrence Street, SW3, in 1745.

Chippendale Furniture: First workshop in St Martin's Lane, WC2.

Fabian Society: Founded in 1884 at 17 Osnaburgh Street, NW1.

Flying Bomb: First fell on London on 13 June 1944 in Grove Road, E3.

Labour Party: Founded on 27 February 1900 on the site of Caroone House, Farringdon Street, EC4.

Millbank Prison: London's largest penitentiary 1816–67, Millbank SW1.

Avro No. 1: The first powered flight by an all-British aircraft took place on Walthamstow Marshes in July 1909; A.V. Roe had built his triplane in the arches of the Walthamstow Marsh Railway Viaduct, E17.

Tyburn Tree: the site of London's most famous gallows, now a traffic island at the junction of Edgware Road and Bayswater Road, W2.

LEISURE: LONDON'S OLDEST CLUBS

Well down from its nineteenth-century peak, clubland has lost more than a few famous institutions over the years but survives nevertheless, its members enjoying some of the most distinguished and elegant buildings in London while the public wanders around outside trying to figure out which is which.

Army & Navy: 37 Pall Mall, SW1 (1837)

Arts Club: 40 Dover Street, W1 (1863)

Athenaeum: 107 Pall Mall, SW1 (1824)

Beefsteak: 9 Irving Street, WC2 (1876)

Boodle's: 28 St James's Street, SW1 (1762)

Brooks's: 60 St James's Street, SW1 (1764)

Buck's: 18 Clifford Street, W1 (1919)

Caledonian: 9 Halkin Street, SW1 (1891)

Carlton: 69 St James's Street, SW1 (1832)

Cavalry & Guards: 127 Piccadilly, W1 (1893)

City Livery: 38 St Mary Axe, EC3 (1914)

City of London: 19 Old Broad Street, EC2 (1832)

City University: 50 Cornhill, EC3 (1895)

East India: 16 St James's Square, SW1 (1849)

Garrick: 15 Garrick Street, WC2 (1831)

National Liberal: Whitehall Place, SW1 (1882)

Naval & Military: 4 St James's Square, SW1 (1862)

Oriental: Stratford Place, W1 (1824)

Oxford & Cambridge: 71 Pall Mall, SW1 (1830)

Pratt's: 14 Park Place, SW1 (1841)

Reform: 104–5 Pall Mall, SW1 (1836)

Royal Air Force: 128 Piccadilly, W1 (1918)

Royal Automobile: 89 Pall Mall, SW1 (1897)

Savage: 1 Whitehall Place, SW1 (1857)

Savile: 69 Brook Street, W1 (1868)

Travellers': 106 Pall Mall, SW1 (1819)

Turf: 5 Carlton House Terrace, SW1 (1868)

White's: 37–8 St James's Street, SW1 (1693)

London's Strangest Museum Exhibits

Hunterian Museum (35–43 Lincoln's Inn Fields, WC2). Housed in the headquarters of the Royal College of Surgeons of England, the museum contains Brien O'Brien's 8ft skeleton and the 'double-headed skull' of a Bengali child.

The National Army Museum (Royal Hospital Road, SW3). No-one knows the whereabouts of Henry VII's most treasured possession – the left leg of St George – but here they've got the bloodied saw used to remove the Marquess of Anglesey's after it was shattered by cannon fire at Waterloo.

London Transport Museum Depot (118–20 Gunnersbury Lane, London W3). An offshoot of the Covent Garden museum, and home to the world's first and last spiral escalator. How it worked, no-one's quite sure.

Horniman Museum (London Road, SE23). A 'torture chair' from the Spanish Inquisition, this fearsome wrought-iron device was said to have come from Cell 23 at Cuenca. In fact it was almost certainly assembled in the nineteenth century, but incorporates an authentic 'garrotte' post which is gruesome enough for most visitors.

Cuming Museum (155 Walworth Road, SE17). London's leading and largest collection of bits and pieces. Exhibits include, for example, a bit of the ceiling of the room where Napoleon died and pieces of the waistcoat worn by Charles I when he was executed.

Marylebone Cricket Club Museum (Lord's, NW8). Besides the disappointingly tiny Ashes trophy, the Club's unrivalled collection of cricket-related memorabilia includes a stuffed bird which was unlucky enough to be struck dead by a well-hit six in the 1930s.

British Museum (Great Russell Street, WC1). Even the experts can be fooled sometimes. On occasional display here is a 'merman' donated by HRH Princess Arthur of Connaught who was told it

had been caught in the Sea of Japan in the eighteenth century. In fact it was cunningly constructed by a fraudster using bits of dried monkey and the tail of a fish.

PECULIARITIES IN LONDON PARKS

Regent's Park has the oldest trees in the capital, a clutch of fossilised stumps by the lake in the Inner Circle. The last surviving remnant of the gardens of the defunct Royal Botanic Society (1839–1932) they were brought from Dorset where a type of conifer tree well-suited to the hot and arid conditions of Jurassic Britain was inundated by hypersaline seawater and preserved in quartz.

Postman's Park, so named because of its proximity to the old General Post Office, contains a unique and moving collection of memorial tablets to otherwise unsung heroes, many of them children, who died attempting to save the lives of others.

As is perhaps only natural for a surviving remnant of the famous Foundling's Hospital, adults are actually banned from the park at Coram's Fields in Bloomsbury, unless they are accompanied by a child.

St James's Park is home to at least one example of every native species of waterfowl (and more besides), hence the ornamental Swiss-style cottage on the lake which was built by the Ornithological

Society of London. With typical Victorian ingenuity it was made steam-heated in order that the members of the Society could assist with the incubation of eggs.

The lack of flowers in Green Park, so named because it is all trees and grass, is ascribed to it having been a burial ground for the adjacent lepers' hospital before this was pulled down to make way for St James's Palace. It used to have two attractive temples, built to mark 100 years of Hanoverian rule, but these were accidentally destroyed by fireworks.

The common at Blackheath was the site of the first golf club in England, laid out in 1608 by James I. Blackheath Rugby Club is similarly the oldest in the UK.

SECRET GARDENS WORTH SEEKING OUT

Chelsea Physic Garden (Swan Walk, SW3). Founded in 1673 for medicinal purposes, by the eighteenth century it had the widest variety of species of any botanical garden anywhere in the world.

College Garden (Westminster Abbey, SW1). Almost certainly the oldest garden in Britain, the ground within the fourteenth-century walls has been under continual cultivation for more than 900 years.

Garden Court (Museum of London, London Wall, EC2). Distinct beds trace the development of plantings from medieval times to the present day.

Grovelands (Southgate Grove, N14). Less well-known than Kenwood, Repton's landscaping is here more clearly visible.

The Roof Gardens (99 Kensington High Street, W8). Constructed on the roof of a former department store in the 1930s, 1½ acres of mature trees and splashing fountains comprise three quite distinct areas: an English woodland garden, a Tudor garden and a Spanish garden.

Tradescant Trust (St Mary's Lambeth, Lambeth Palace Road, SE1). Together with a collection of Tradescantia, the churchyard has been reworked as a scholarly re-creation of a seventeenth-century garden.

Trinity Hospital (Highbridge, SE10). Two acres of ancient cloisters, mulberry trees and wisteria surround this charming building erected amid orchards as early as 1617.

THEATRELAND: THE TEN-MINUTE TOUR

Adelphi, The Strand, WC2
The name means 'brothers' but the original theatre was built in 1806 for the owner's daughter, stage-struck Jane Scott taking the lead in Miss Scott's Entertainments. In 1834 it acquired Britain's first mechanically sinking stage, and was where Alan Jay Lerner allowed his seventh wife to play the lead in *My Fair Lady*.

Albery, St Martin's Lane, WC2
Originally the New Theatre, when it was no longer new it was renamed after Sir Bronson Albery, son of the original founder, a drunk who died of cirrhosis of the liver. It was home to the Old Vic and Sadlers Wells when both were bombed during the war.

Aldwych, Strand, WC2
A club for Australian servicemen in the First World War, it subsequently gained fame for its 'Aldwych Farces' and for twenty-two years was home to the Royal Shakespeare Company. It was also the venue for the RSC's version of *Nicholas Nickleby* which ran for nearly nine hours.

Apollo, Shaftesbury Avenue, W1
The first theatre of the Edwardian age, the Apollo opened just four weeks after the death of Queen Victoria. The smallest of the four theatres on Shaftesbury Avenue, it was built mostly to stage musicals.

Apollo Victoria, Wilton Road, SW1
Unusual in that it was originally a 'picture palace', opening as such in 1930 and only converting to a theatre half a century later, thereby reversing the usual trend.

Cambridge, Earlham Street, WC2
The second of six West End theatres to open in a single year (1930), its fashionable silver and gold decor didn't age well and was eventually painted over. Happily the female nudes at the entrance remained untouched.

Coliseum, St Martin's Lane, WC2
Its spinning globe dominating a busy corner of London, this gigantic Edwardian edifice opened in 1904, withstood two direct hits during the Second World War and has subsequently provided a home for the English National Opera.

Criterion, Piccadilly Circus, SW1
Unpopular when it opened in 1874 (forced air pumps were needed to prevent patrons from suffocating), its fortunes subsequently recovered, although being underground it was badly flooded in 1985.

Dominion, Tottenham Court Road, W1
Originally a theatre, but later converted to a cinema, the Dominion underwent a renaissance in 1986 as the home of the space-age musical *Time* with its much-vaunted special effects and technical wizardry.

Duke of York's, St Martin's Lane, WC2
When it opened in 1882 St Martin's Lane was literally a lane, with the small playhouse originally run as the Trafalgar. *Peter Pan* made its debut here in 1904, 14-year-old Noel Coward appearing in another performance of it just nine years later.

Fortune, Russell Street, WC2
Sharing its building with the Scottish National Church, considerable confusion must have ensued when the theatre first opened for business with a play called *The Sinners*.

Garrick, Charing Cross Road, WC2
Funded by W.S. Gilbert, the theatre opened exactly 110 years after the great actor's death, its opening having been delayed somewhat when the builders hit an underground river which had been lost since Roman times.

Her Majesty's, Haymarket, SW1
Now dwarfed by New Zealand House, the theatre was briefly the Italian Opera House – hence the Royal Opera Arcade behind – and is traditionally renamed His or Hers each time a monarch of the opposite sex ascends the throne.

London Palladium, Argyll Street, W1

Replacing Charles Hengler's Circus, and using some of its materials in its impressive façade, the vast, golden auditorium formed a backdrop to a succession of 'Live from the Palladium' television spectaculars over a period lasting more than thirty years. Unusually it used to feature telephone connections from box to box.

Lyric, Shaftesbury Avenue, W1

For years comic operas were the main fare here, one such (*Dorothy*) running for 817 performances before being replaced by the next one (*Doris*), presumably in a similar vein. More recently Leonard Rossiter dropped dead in the middle of a performance, starring in a production of Joe Orton's *Loot* complete with a coffin at centre stage.

New Ambassadors, West Street, WC2

Home to *The Mousetrap* for its first twenty-odd years, although one suspects few tourists taking their seats in the stalls realise Agatha Christie borrowed this title from Shakespeare.

New London, Drury Lane, WC2

Built in 1973, close to the site of The Mogul, a celebrated pub-cum-music hall having held performances by Dan Leno, Marie Lloyd and others. The West End's newest theatre it was home to *Cats* for years and years and years.

Novello, Aldwych, WC2

Bombed in not one but two world wars, as the Strand it was the scene of a record-breaking run (for a farce) with the iconic *No Sex Please, We're British*.

Old Vic, The Cut, Waterloo Road, SE1

Originally a 'house of melodrama', in 1820 a new curtain was devised which comprised sixty-three large pieces of mirrored glass. Unfortunately the weight was too much for the roof and it had to come down, despite being a huge draw for audiences.

Palace, Cambridge Circus, W1

Built by Richard D'Oyly Carte in 1891 as the Royal English Opera House, the place had high ideals but a short life before becoming a conventional theatre. It was eventually rescued by Andrew Lloyd Webber and a succession of massive box-office successes.

Phoenix, Charing Cross Road, W1
Just four days in the writing (he had 'flu at the time) Noel Coward's *Brief Lives* was the first play staged at the Phoenix, the star a relative unknown called Laurence Olivier aged twenty-three.

Piccadilly, Denman Street, W1
When it opened in 1928, the promoters boasted that had they laid every brick used in its construction end to end they would have stretched from London to Paris. Which may have been true since, with 1,400 seats, this is still one of the largest auditoriums in London.

Prince Edward, Old Compton Street, W1
First a draper's shop, then a theatre, a casino-restaurant, a servicemen's club and then a cinema . . . the owners must have thought the site was doomed until, finally, they found *Evita* (1978–86) and security of tenure.

Prince of Wales, Coventry Street, W1
With its new building opening in October 1937, within a few short years Mae West was treading the boards here, also James Stewart, thereby pre-empting the current trend for Hollywood stars in the West End by a good half-century. It was briefly run by Edith Evans.

Queen's, Shaftesbury Avenue, W1
Its Louis XVI interior providing a stark contrast with its plate-glass and brick façade, for a short while the Queen's hosted tea dances and was all but destroyed in the Blitz.

Royal Opera House, Bow Street, Covent Garden, WC2
Less opulent or monumental than either La Scala or the Paris Opera, the Royal Opera House has nevertheless managed to secure an unwanted reputation for extravagance.

St Martin's, West Street, WC2
Home to *The Mousetrap* for so long it's hard to imagine that anything else ever played here. Nice wood-panelled interior, though.

Savoy, Strand, WC2

As *The Times* reported at the time (1881): 'This is the first time that it has been attempted to light any public building entirely by electricity. What is being done is an experiment, and may succeed or fail.'

Shaftesbury, 210 Shaftesbury Avenue, WC2

First the New Prince's, then in 1914 the Prince's, what eventually became the Shaftesbury hosted everything from Gilbert & Sullivan to Diaghilev and *Hair* before being taken over by the popular Theatre of Comedy company.

Theatre Royal, Drury Lane, Catherine Street, WC2

London's oldest and most historic theatre, being the latest incarnation of a playhouse which opened on the site in 1662. Charles II was a big fan, granting the players their own livery as part of the Royal Household, a unique privilege for a London theatre.

Theatre Royal Haymarket, Haymarket, SW1

The third theatre in London to get a patent to perform legitimate theatre, but only because the owner lost a leg after being thrown from the Duke of York's horse in 1766 and the Duke felt sorry for him.

Vaudeville, Strand, WC2

Originally built for three actors-owners – Messrs James, Montague and Thorne (aka the Jew, the Gent and the Gentile) – it was from the Vaudeville that Henry Irving launched his career.

Whitehall, Whitehall, SW1

A ghostly white tombstone of a building, the Whitehall made its mark during the Second World War with a 'non-stop revue' featuring the stripper Phyllis Dixey. Non-stop, that is, from 2pm to 9pm daily.

7

DEATH & RELIGION

TEN BIZARRE FACTS ABOUT WESTMINSTER ABBEY

When it was built by Edward the Confessor the Abbey was on a remote island called Thorney Island (or the isle of thorns) situated in the middle of some unpromising marshland well to the west of London.

As a major religious centre in the Middle Ages, Westminster Abbey had its fair share of holy relics. These included the Virgin Mary's girdle and St Peter's vestments, hair from Mary Magdalene, a phial of Christ's blood, the very stones used to pummel St Stephen to death, St Benedict's head and a tooth from one of the three Wise Men.

As a so-called Royal Peculiar, making it exempt from the jurisdiction of the diocese in which it stands, it is technically neither a church nor a cathedral. To a large degree this explains why so many of the monuments survived the Dissolution in 1540.

Following the Dissolution a proportion of the Abbey's immense revenues were transferred to St Paul's Cathedral, thus explaining the origin of the phrase 'robbing Peter to pay Paul'.

In 1653 an individual known only as Old Parr was buried at the Abbey at the reputed age of 152. He was accorded this rare honour by Charles I who was delighted to have met the oldest man in the world.

During the Civil War Cromwell's men actually set up camp in the Abbey, breaking up and burning many of the fixtures. Little wonder that, while he and several Puritan leaders were later interred in the Abbey, at the Restoration their bodies were dug up and gibbetted.

To ensure that the body in the Tomb of the Unknown Warrior would remain truly unknown six bodies were exhumed from the battlefields at Ypres, Arras, Cambrai, the Aisne, the Marne and the Somme and taken to a hut at St Pol. Once the authorities were satisfied that all six were British, a Brigadier-General Wyatt entered the hut, blindfold and at midnight, and picked one at random. To commemorate the First World War Allies, the Unknown Warrior's coffin of English oak is surrounded by French soil and sealed beneath a funeral slab of Belgian black marble.

Traces of human skin can still be seen nailed to the small door opposite St Faith's Chapel. The door gives on to the Pyx, a small chamber where the Abbey's treasures were once stored, and as a gruesome warning to others the skin was flayed from a fourteenth-century thief who was executed after attempting to steal the valuables.

Many of the poets commemorated in Poets' Corner are not actually buried there as the authorities of the day found their unconventional lives unacceptable. Shakespeare for example had to wait until 1740 for his memorial, and William Blake until 1957, the bicentenary of his birth. Space was found for Ben Jonson, however, but only 4sq ft, so he is buried standing up.

The first public building ever to be vacuumed (just in time for Edward VII's coronation in 1901) the Abbey was cleaned from top to bottom using 'Puffing Billy', Herbert Cecil Booth's latest invention, which featured a small 5hp electric motor sucking air through a cloth filter.

TEN STRANGE THINGS ABOUT ST PAUL'S

The building we see today is actually the fifth St Paul's, the original having been built around AD 604 on the remains of a Roman temple dedicated to Diana.

Old St Paul's, the medieval cathedral destroyed in the Great Fire, was not only 124ft taller than Sir Christopher Wren's replacement but also considerably longer and wider. In the thirteenth century it even contained its own law school – until Henry III banned the teaching of law in the City in a bid to boost the prestige of his new foundations at Oxford – and two separate prisons housed in the twin bell towers. Indeed St Paul's was so large that the cathedral authorities tried to institute laws forbidding Londoners to use it as a short cut from one side of the city to the other.

The only monument to survive the fire was that of the poet, preacher and Dean John Donne. Many remnants have been preserved in the cathedral's Lapidarium, however, including stonework dating from the Norman era right through to the Renaissance portico added by Inigo Jones. Sir Nicholas Bacon's top half can also be seen in the crypt, badly scorched by the flames.

Demolishing the ruin of the Old St Paul's turned out to be such a daunting task – three labourers fell to their deaths in the first couple of weeks, and Pepys records feeling sea-sick at the sight of them working – that one of Wren's first innovations was a new type of steel-tipped battering-ram powered by thirty men. In the end, however, he had to send to the Tower for gunpowder and blow it to bits.

Wren's new St Paul's was intended to double up as a giant scientific instrument. Wearing one of his other hats (he was Professor of Astronomy at Gresham College, and then at Oxford) he had already experimented in the old building with pendulums and in 1704 proposed building the south-west staircase in his new St Paul's in such a manner as to provide a stable mount for a massive 123ft tubeless telescope.

Grinling Gibbons, England's pre-eminent carver in oak and limewood, worked on the cathedral from 1695 to 1699. His talents were recognised only by accident, when he was spotted while working at a shipyard. Peering through cottage windows while out walking one evening, John Evelyn observed the young Gibbons at work and rushed off to tell his friends Wren and Pepys about his discovery, and later Charles II.

By far the most expensive building of its age, the total cost for St Paul's came to a staggering £747,661 10s – this at a time when a labourer working on the site would have been earning less than 2s a day. Much of the money came from a newly imposed Coal Tax, although typically the 'temporary' tax wasn't rescinded until 1889.

Thirty-five years in all, the building took so long to complete that the House of Commons, irritated by innumerable delays, slashed Wren's salary by half (to just £100 per annum) and Wren himself grew so old that towards the end he was unable to climb the scaffolding and had to be hauled up in a basket.

Contrary to the popular rumour Nelson's body isn't in the gilded ball on the top of the cathedral but down below in the crypt. Brought back to England preserved in a barrel of spirits, it was sealed in a coffin made from timber from the mainmast of *L'Orient* and placed in a magnificent porphyry sarcophagus originally intended for Cardinal Wolsey. (*L'Orient*, the French flagship, sank at the Battle of the Nile after being blown up, an incident recorded on the nearby monument to George Blagdon Westcott, Captain of the *Majestic*.)

In 1796 the cathedral organist was Thomas Attwood who had trained under Mozart. Spotting a unique talent in the young Mendelssohn thirty-odd years later, he invited him to play in St Paul's but when the vergers became exasperated at the size of the crowd who came in to listen they let the air out of the organ and shooed everyone out.

CHURCHES WITH CURIOUS NAMES

St Andrew by the Wardrobe – the adjoining King's Wardrobe was a store for royal ceremonial garments until it was razed in the Great Fire. (Queen Victoria Street, EC4)

St Antholin – the name derives from Anthony the Hermit. (Nunhead Lane, SE15)

St Benet Sherehog – a sherehog is a ram castrated after its first shearing. St Benet seems to have attracted all the best names, St Benet Fink in Threadneedle Street being named after Robert Fink who paid for the building. (Both demolished)

St Clement Danes – the church where invading Danes were buried, say some authorities; or possibly the one that those married to English women were permitted to use after their fellows had been driven out of the country. (Strand, WC2)

St Giles without Cripplegate – although the origin of the name Cripplegate is obscure, St Giles was to become the patron saint of cripples. (Fore Street, EC2)

St James Garlickhythe – it seems absurdly specialised for any wharf, but John Stow in 1598 confirmed that garlic was sold nearby. A peculiarity of the church was a corpse in a glass coffin, known as 'Jimmy Garlick'. (Garlick Hill, EC4)

St Katherine Cree – 'cree' is thought to be a corruption of Christ Church. For more than 350 years the incumbent has preached a so-called Lion Service every 16 October giving thanks for a Lord Mayor who met a lion in Syria and survived to tell the tale. (Leadenhall Street, EC3)

St Margaret Pattens – pattens, rough wooden platform soles designed to keep one's shoes out of the mud, were manufactured nearby. (Rood Lane, EC3)

St Mary Abchurch – meaning 'up church' as it was upriver from the neighbouring priory. (Abchurch Yard, EC4)

St Mary Axe – recalls a legend about a princess who travelled abroad with her 11,000 handmaidens. All were killed by Attila, using three axes, one of which was preserved in the church. (Now demolished)

St Mary Woolnoth – built on the site of a Roman temple, by a Saxon lord Wulfnoth. (Lombard Street, EC4)

St Michael Paternoster Royal – far from denoting anything regal, 'royal' is a corruption of the French town of La Reole from where local vintners sourced their supplies of Bordeaux wines. (College Hill, EC4)

St Olave – Olaf was a Norwegian who fought the Danes alongside Ethelred the Unready and was canonised in 1025 for this service to Christianity.

St Peter ad Vincula – literally St Peter in chains, which is appropriate as the chapel was founded in the twelfth century for prisoners in the Tower. When Queen Victoria ordered that the floor be taken up and the bodies given a decent burial 200 were discovered, including that of Anne Boleyn. (Tower Green, EC3)

St Sepulchre without Newgate – at the time of the Crusades the church which is now the largest in the City was called St Edmund and the Holy Sepulchre. This was eventually contracted to St Sepulchre, although there is no saint of this name. (Giltspur Street, EC1)

St Vedast alias Foster – a sixth-century bishop in northern Gaul, Vedast helped to restore Christianity to the region after decades of destruction at the hands of barbarians. (Foster Lane, EC2)

THE EXTRAORDINARY INDUSTRY OF CHRISTOPHER WREN

St Paul's Cathedral, Emmanuel College Chapel at Cambridge, the Upper School at Eton, his work at Hampton Court Palace and the Royal Observatory, the Monument, the Royal Hospital and Royal Naval Hospital and countless other buildings scattered throughout London and the shires. Yet Wren still found time to build or rebuild a staggering fifty-one City churches (and others elsewhere in London) – for which he was paid not a penny. Fate, however, has not dealt kindly with them all.

Intact:
St Benet, Paul's Wharf
St Clement Danes, Strand
St Clement, Eastcheap
St James, Garlick Hill
St Margaret, Lothbury
St Margaret Pattens
St Martin, Ludgate
St Mary Abchurch
St Mary Aldermary Tower, Bow Lane
St Michael, Cornhill
St Peter, Cornhill
St Stephen, Walbrook

Restored after the Blitz:
St Andrew by the Wardrobe
St Andrew, Holborn
St Anne and St Agnes, Gresham Street
St Bride, Fleet Street
St Edmund King and Martyr, Lombard Street
St Lawrence, Jewry
St Mary-le-Bow, Cheapside
St Mary-at-Hill, Thames Street

St Michael Paternoster Royal, College Hill
St Nicholas, Cole Abbey
St Vedast-alias-Foster, Foster Lane

Gone for Good
All Hallows the Great, Upper Thames Street – demolished
All Hallows, Bread Street – demolished
All Hallows, Lombard Street – demolished
St Antholin, Watling Street – demolished
St Augustine, Watling Street – bombed
St Bartholomew, Exchange – demolished
St Benet Fink, Threadneedle Street – demolished
St Benet, Gracechurch Street – demolished
St Christopher-le-Stocks, Threadneedle Street – demolished
St Dionis Backchurch, Fenchurch Street – demolished
St George, Botolph Lane – demolished
St Magnus Martyr, Lower Thames Street – substantially altered
St Mary Magdalene, Fish Street (gutted by fire)
St Mary, Aldermanbury – shipped to Fulton, Missouri
St Matthew, Friday Street – demolished
St Michael, Bassishaw – demolished
St Michael, Crooked Lane – demolished
St Michael, Queenhithe – demolished
St Michael, Wood Street – demolished
St Mildred, Bread Street – bombed
St Mildred, Poultry – demolished
St Stephen, Coleman Street – bombed
St Swithin, Cannon Street – bombed

Nothing Left but the Tower
Christ Church, Newgate Street
St Alban, Wood Street
St Anne's Church, Soho
St Dunstan in the East
St Mary Somerset, Thames Street
St Olave, Old Jewry

NINE SAINTS' DAYS WITH LONDON ASSOCIATIONS

25 February: Sebert (664–94), an East Saxon king who converted his people and who, though buried in the original St Paul's Cathedral in a coffin which reputedly grew to accommodate his tall frame, is said by some to have founded the first monastery on Thorney Island, Westminster.

4 May: John Houghton (1487–1533) was hanged, drawn and quartered for 'treacherously machinating and desiring' to deprive Henry VIII of his position as head of the church. One quarter was nailed over the gate at the Charterhouse where he had formerly been Prior.

19 May: Dunstan (909–88). A Benedictine Bishop of London and Archbishop of Canterbury, Dunstan revived monastic traditions following the Danes' withdrawal and was granted a charter from Edgar authorising the building of Westminster Abbey.

21 June: Thomas More (1478–1535) refused to submit to the Act of Succession and as a consequence was executed at the Tower. His body was buried there, in St Peter ad Vincula, while his head was eventually removed to Canterbury.

22 June: John Fisher (1469–1535) was another martyr who suffered a similar fate at a similar time, and for similar reasons. However, while his body too was buried at the Tower his head was displayed on a pole on London Bridge and then dumped in the river.

20 July: Uncumber (date unknown) was crucified by her own father after growing a beard in order to deter suitors after she had taken a vow of chastity. Uncumber has a carved likeness in the Henry VIII Chapel at Westminster, and is also known as Wilgefort.

13 October: Edward the Confessor (1003–66), England's only albino king, he did much to promote the primacy of Westminster Abbey, laying the foundations for it to become the place for coronations and many centuries of royal burials.

25 October: John Southworth (1592–1654), a priest who was condemned to death under Charles I and then again by Cromwell. Having aided victims of the plague, Southworth's body was purchased from the hangman by the King of Portugal to be honoured in the Chapel of St George and the English Martyrs at Westminster's Catholic cathedral.

31 October: Melitus (d. 624), the first Bishop of London (and third Archbishop of Canterbury), he arrived in England in 601, as an emissary of Pope Gregory, shortly after which time the first cathedral dedicated to St Paul was built in the city, possibly on the site of a Roman temple.

SYNAGOGUES, MOSQUES AND OTHER TEMPLES OF DELIGHT

The mosque in Fournier Street, E1, was previously a synagogue, prior to this a Methodist chapel and before that a Huguenot one, having been built for this purpose in 1743.

The first synagogue to be built in London after Cromwell readmitted the Jews was in Creechurch Street, but the oldest still standing is the Spanish and Portuguese Synagogue of 1701 in Bevis Marks, EC3.

With its burnished gold onion dome visible from the M4 as it crosses the Chiswick Flyover, London's first Russian Orthodox Cathedral opened its doors in 2000.

At least 140ft tall, Sir Frederick Gibberd's shimmering London Central Mosque in Regent's Park was only completed in 1978 despite the fact that the Nizam of Hyderabad had launched a building fund for it in the 1920s and the Crown Estate had made the site available twenty years later.

Neasden's sensational Shri Swaminarayan Hindu temple was built entirely by volunteers, an estimated 2,000 of them piecing together many thousands of tons of Italian marble, Bulgarian limestone and teak. Much of this had been first shipped to India to be carved by 1,500 craftsmen, carefully numbered and then shipped back to north-west London. The cost was met in part by the largest drinks-can recycling campaign ever seen in the UK.

London's largest collection of Buddhas is in Soho's Fo Guang Temple, the former All Saints' Church, Margaret Street, which in the 1830s had been the headquarters of the High Church Tractarian Society.

Now the centre of Britain's Armenian community, the St Arkis Church in Iverna Garden, W8, was commissioned in 1922 by the oil magnate Calouste Gulbenkian as a memorial to his parents. Said by the 1950s to be the richest man in the world – hence the fact that his church was designed by the architects of the Ritz, Mewes and Davis – Gulbenkian himself died in 1955, alone in a hotel room in Lisbon.

ROCKERS WHO CONKED OUT IN (OR NEAR) LONDON

Marc Bolan (1977) A mod-cum-model before discovering flower power, Hackney-born Mark Feld was killed in a crash when the Mini driven by his girlfriend hit a tree on Queen's Ride, Barnes.

Graham Bond (1974) Mellotron pioneer and leader of the eponymous Organisation, drugs and an interest in the occult eventually led to his mysterious death beneath the wheels of a train at Finsbury Park.

John 'Bonzo' Bonham (1980) Despite owning the Boston Strangler, a V8-engined Model-T Ford reputed at the time to be the fastest hot-rod outside the USA, the Led Zeppelin drummer died of asphyxiation at his home in Windsor after an all-day drinking binge.

Tara Browne (1966) Groovy designer son of Lord Oranmore and Browne, the young honourable perished in perfect 1960s fashion in a trendy sky-blue Lotus Elan in Chelsea's Redcliffe Gardens. He was immortalised by the Beatles as the man who 'blew his mind out in a car' in 'A Day in the Life'.

Eddie Cochrane (1960) Dead at twenty-one, his iconic status was ensured when it was noted with macabre fascination that the single topping the UK charts at the time was his 'Three Steps to Heaven'. He died on the way to Heathrow Airport when a teenage minicab driver lost control.

Desmond Dekker (2006) The Ska legend and honorary 'Israelite' lived for many years in a maisonette in south London's Forest Hill.

Sandy Denny (1978) A hugely talented singer-songwriter with Fairport Convention, Sandy struck out solo but missed her footing on the stairs and died of a cerebral haemorrhage.

Cass Elliot (1974) Great voice, but always overweight, she collapsed and died of a heart attack in Harry Nilsson's Mayfair flat.

Brian Epstein (1967) The erstwhile manager of the Beatles died of an accidental overdose. 'We'd never have made it without him', admitted John Lennon.

Jimi Hendrix (1970) The singer and iconic guitarist was dead on arrival at St Mary Abbot's Hospital, having overdosed and choked on his own vomit.

Jimmy McCulloch (1979) Guitarist for the underrated Thunderclap Newman (and Paul McCartney's Wings) died of heart failure.

Freddie Mercury (1991) Queen's extraordinary Zoroastrian front man died from complications arising from AIDS.

Keith Moon (1978) The wildest of wild drummers, frequently brilliant but reliably unreliable, the Who's trap-rattler overdosed in the same block as Cass Elliot.

Keith Relf (1976) The Yardbirds guitarist was electrocuted by his own instrument.

Bon Scott (1980) The AC/DC vocalist succumbed to acute alcohol poisoning.

Screaming Lord Sutch (1999) The original Official Monster Raving Loony and erstwhile rock star was found hanged at home, apparently having committed suicide.

EIGHT INTRIGUING LONDON MEMORIALS

At the army church of St Mary Magdalene at Woolwich in south-east London, a plaque states the following:

> Sacred to the Memory of Major James Brush
> Who was killed by the accidental discharge of a pistol by
> his orderly 14th April 1831
> Well done, o good and faithful servant.

A larger plaque in the same church records the death of five young children, all of whom drowned tragically while 'amusing themselves on the ice of Bowater Pond on Sunday, the 6th of February 1831.' Chillingly it continues:

> caused this memorial to be erected . . . to impress upon
> the young the necessity and importance of remembering
> their creator [and] to avoid the sin and danger of
> violating the Sabbath Day.

At Kensal Green the headstone for composer Henry Russell (1812–1900) is in the form of a mammoth stone armchair, and his epitaph finishes with the words

> I love it, I love it and who shall dare
> To chide me for loving this old armchair.

The burial register at Shoreditch in the East End records the death of Thomas Cam, easily London's oldest old-boy at the age of 207.

At Brompton Cemetery the family of Alfred John Priddell (who died in 1942) spoke for many when they put the following on his stone:

> The call was so sudden, the shock severe.
> We never thought your end so near.

St Bartholomew the Great, EC1, London's oldest church, contains a touching memorial to Mr and Mrs John Whiting, dated 1681:

> Shee first deceased, hee for a little tryd
> To live without her, lik'd it not and dyd.

A headstone at St Michael's, Crooked Lane, in 1831 recorded the fact that:

> Here lyeth wrapped in clay
> The body of William Wray
> I have no more to say.

And back at St Leonard, Shoreditch, another one, briefer still:

> Exit Burbage, 1619.

Enough said.

ELEVEN LONDON GHOSTS

In Westminster Abbey it is said that after the crowds have dispersed on Armistice Day a uniformed figure has been observed to materialise by the Tomb of the Unknown Warrior, head bowed in

sorrow at his own fate and that of his dead comrades. A so-called floating monk has also been seen hovering a foot or two above the floor here, and in the 1930s actually engaged a couple of American tourists in conversation.

Unsurprisingly the Tower of London is one of the ghost-hunter's richest hunting grounds and as long ago as the thirteenth century labourers working here claimed that the ghost of St Thomas Becket had twice destroyed their work with a sweep of his crozier. Each year on 21 May the ghost of the hapless Henry VI is also said to pace up and down the Wakefield Tower marking the anniversary of his murder.

Perhaps the most unnerving though is the mysterious, murmuring yellow glow which has been reported in the nearby Salt Tower. Accompanied by a touch 'like cold fingers on the back of the neck', the phenomenon has been attributed to Henry Walpole, a Jesuit who was viciously tortured here on the orders of Henry VIII.

Somewhat less expected, however, is to discover a ghost on the Tube, not far from the Tower. Staff at Aldgate station have been keeping a log of such incidents since the 1950s. In one report a maintenance worker is said to have survived a 22,000 volt shock from the third rail, immediately after a colleague had observed what he took to be a grey-haired figure, presumably his guardian angel, gently stroking his hair.

Thirty years later another equally mysterious figure made herself known when a photographer visited St Botolph's Without Bishops-gate. Developing the film in his home darkroom he found that in one picture she could be seen gazing down at him from the gallery. Surprised, as he knew the only other person in the building at the time was his wife, he was later contacted by a builder who, working in the crypt, claimed to have dislodged the lid of a coffin revealing the well-preserved face of a woman whose description closely matched the pale apparition in the photograph.

Still in the City, the magnificent precincts of the Bank of England are haunted by an old lady of their own. Dressed in black and nicknamed 'the Bank Nun' she's the spirit of Sarah Whitehead who, refusing to acknowledge the death of a sibling executed for forgery in 1812, visited the bank every day for years, enquiring of counter staff, 'Have you seen my brother?'

Across town the decorated sarcophagi and mummies make the British Museum's Egyptian Galleries one of its most popular areas, but also its most haunted. Here a spirit connected with an exhibit labelled only as 'Unnamed singer of Amen-Re' is believed to have put a curse on all its future keepers. One disappeared without trace, a second was wounded in a shooting accident, and a third, fearing for his life, sold it to an antiquary after which a porter carrying it into the museum himself dropped dead. Quite a tally, although nothing more has been heard from it since an exorcism was carried out by two psychics in 1921.

Further south Lord Nelson's ghost has been observed crossing the great quadrangle at Somerset House, although it never enters the building. And in St James's Park witnesses have reported a headless woman rising out of the water before running into the nearby bushes. She's the wife of a guardsman, apparently, who hacked off her head and slipped her body into the lake.

TIRED OF LONDON:
GRISLY DEATHS & SPECTACULAR SUICIDES

Thomas Beale died in 1816, having (according to his monument at St Mary's, Battersea) 'burned to death on a limekiln at Nine Elms'.

Chung Ling-Su, a self-styled Chinese magician whose real name was William Ellisworth Robinson, died in 1918 at the Empire, Wood Green, after attempting to catch a bullet between his teeth.

In 1774 the great Clive of India died a lonely death, from laudanum, at his house in Berkeley Square.

To the horror of onlookers Albert Smart, a watchmaker, threw himself off the Whispering Gallery in St Paul's Cathedral in March 1856.

Twelve years later Thomas Lee hurled himself off the North Tower of the Crystal Palace.

John William Godward, a painter in the tradition of Lord Leighton and Sir Lawrence Alma-Tadema if not quite in the same class, in 1922 succeeded in burning his own head off in a domestic oven.

Literally an artist starving in his garret, in 1685 the playwright Thomas Otway was given some bread by a well-meaning friend but choked on it and died.

BAD TIMES: 12 YEARS IN WHICH TO QUIT THE CITY

61   With Colchester the Roman capital, but London an
      important commercial centre, the old city was razed by Iceni
      Queen Boudicca and the population forced to flee ahead of
      the arrival of Roman troops to restore order.

401   Following repeated raids, and the Romans' withdrawal to
      defend their empire, London's population began to drift
      away, the Thames quays silted up and economic activity in
      the city steadily ground to a halt.

1212 Large scale conflagrations were not uncommon in London, but
      the one was particularly bad – one medieval report suggests
      3,000 dead (compared to just nine in the so-called Great Fire
      four centuries later) – and led to new laws requiring the use of
      brick and tile for rebuilding rather than wood and thatch.

1348 In November of that year the Black Death struck London.
      Killing half the population of England, the proportion
      affected in the city was even greater as crowded streets helped
      it spread faster and further.

1381 Revolting peasants marched on London, a teenage Richard II
      sought refuge in the Tower, prisons were opened, palaces
      ransacked and burned, and the Archbishop of Canterbury
      was beheaded. Also scores of lawyers, so it wasn't all bad.

1664 Up to 100,000 Londoners died of dropsy, griping of the guts,
      wind, worms and the French Pox – but in reality of the Great
      Plague. Servants dismissed by anxious employers looted
      empty houses, and manufacturing in the city collapsed as
      Newcastle colliers refused to deliver fuel into London.

1666 Only nine people died in the Great Fire, but among the
      destroyed premises were 87 churches, more than 40 livery
      halls, 13,200 domestic dwellings with a total of 463 acres laid
      waste. Incredibly the vast majority had been rebuilt and
      reoccupied within six years.

1780 The Gordon Riots, originally merely an anti-Catholic march
      on Parliament, quickly became a general, all-purpose orgy of
      looting and burning. Five prisons were wrecked, a gin
      distillery breached which didn't help matters, and then the

Bank of England was attacked. Up to 850 died in the process, with the 21 ringleaders being hanged once order was restored.

1858   Cholera was endemic in London but it took a combination of a hot summer, unusually dry weather and a network of sewers disgorging into the Thames before the resulting 'Great Stink' finally forced the authorities – with the help of Sir Joseph Bazalgette – to do something about it.

1918   With the citizenry already weakened by the First World War, a flu pandemic swept around the world killing more than 220,000 Britons. London was especially hard hit with its densely packed population transmitting the deadly virus more efficiently.

1940   A combination of Blitz and blackout devastated London, the former killing 15,000 – 1,436 on a single night – and damaging or destroying an incredible 3.5 million buildings. At the same time the latter provided cover for an unprecedented crime wave – a feature overlooked by many books extolling the virtues of the wartime spirit – and the country's highest ever traffic casualty figures.

1952   A frequent problem in London before the Clean Air Act of 1956 – in 1813 impenetrable fog descended on the capital and didn't clear for seven days – in December 1952 with sulphur dioxide combining with rainwater and oxygen to form deadly sulphuric acid up to 4,000 residents died together with scores of cattle at Smithfield Market.

8

FOOD & DRINK

THE WEIRDEST MEALS EVER EATEN IN LONDON

In 1862 Francis Buckland's inaugural dinner of the Society for the Acclimatisation of Animals in the United Kingdom featured Japanese sea-slug soup, porpoise heads (boiled and fried), rhino pie, panther cutlets, kangaroo steaks and stew, and savouries of mice on toast. His intention was to bring new dishes to the public's notice, in order to alleviate occasional food shortages, but after a dinner of horse tongue, soup and sausage at the Langham Hotel, he admitted that 'hippophagy has not the slightest chance of success in this country'.

His father William meanwhile, the Dean of Westminster, claimed to be able to identify wherever he was simply by tasting the topsoil, also that boiled mole was the most disgusting thing he had ever tasted – at least until he tried a bluebottle. Years later, when the

Archbishop of York showed him Louis XIV's embalmed heart, a treasured souvenir, William Buckland popped it in whole saying, 'I've eaten most things, but never the heart of a king'.

Sir George Reresby Sitwell Bt who banned electricity from his home until well into the 1940s and tried to pay his son's school fees in pigs and potatoes, attempted to get Selfridge's food hall to stock his 'Sitwell Egg'. This appalling-sounding portable meal comprised a yolk of smoked meat, compressed-rice white and a shell of artificial lime; Gordon Selfridge was not surprisingly not impressed.

LONDON'S BIGGEST BLOW-OUTS

Edward III's son, the Duke of Clarence, once threw a banquet for 10,000 subjects which comprised thirty separate courses; Richard II routinely employed an estimated 2,000 kitchen staff to cope with his culinary demands; and at the coronation of Henry V the conduits of Palace Yard, Whitehall, were said literally to have run with claret.

In 1531 Ely House, Holborn, played host to an immense five-day banquet for Henry VIII and Catherine of Aragon, at which were consumed 100 sheep, 51 cows and 24 oxen, 91 pigs, 444 pigeons, 168 swans, 720 chickens and a staggering 4,000 larks.

Henry VI came to the throne aged just eight months old, and at his coronation feast leopards were allegedly immersed in custard and lions allowed to swim in the soup.

Ye Olde Cheshire Cheese in Fleet Street was once celebrated for its famous pie weighing between 50 and 80lb. 'Entombed therein', reported one lucky enough to have tried it, 'were beefsteaks, kidneys, oysters, larks, mushrooms and wondrous spices and gravies, the secret of which is known only to the compounder.' It is said that on a breezy day the aroma carried as far as the Stock Exchange.

The greatest banquet of them all, however, must have been that given by the Earl of Warwick for the Duke of York in 1470. A manuscript discovered at the Tower of London, and cited by the great chef Alexis Soyer, describes 1,577 kitchen and serving staff despatching:

108,560 pints of wine, 840 of them spiced

504,000 pints of ale

6,000 custards, hot and cold

5,000 woodcocks

4,155 venison pasties, hot and cold

4,000 each of roebuck, buck and doe

4,000 each of pigeon, duck and rabbit

3,000 calves

2,000 chickens

1,004 withers or rams

1,000 jellies

1,000 egrets

500 partridge

400 tarts

400 each of plover, hernsie or heron

300 pigs and 300 hogs

300 each of capon, pike, bream

204 bitterns

200 young goats

200 each of pheasant, crane, and cree or sandpiper

100 each of peacock, curlew and quail

10 fat oxen

8 seals

6 wild bulls

4 porpoises

EXTRAORDINARY VENUES FOR DINNER

Fleet Prison: despite being consigned to this hellhole in 1596 for various financial irregularities Richard Stoneley, an official of the Exchequer, regularly entertained his wife and family in his cell where they enjoyed a calf's head, roast veal, boiled beef, and small gamebirds. Followed by cheese and fruit, their splendid dinner would be accompanied by plenty of claret and 'canary sack' or dry white wine.

Boating at the Savoy: in 1905 American millionaire George A. Kessler entertained two dozen guests with a giant, flower-laden gondola floating in the flooded courtyard of the Savoy Hotel. With the courtyard painted to resemble Venice, a giant birthday cake arriving on the back of an elephant and Caruso singing 'Happy Birthday', the occasion was marred only by a quantity of dead swans which had been killed off by a toxic blue dye introduced into the hotel's temporary lagoon.

Looking down on Trafalgar Square: to celebrate the long overdue erection of a monument to Nelson in October 1843 – Britain's naval hero had been dead for more than half a century by the time Landseer's lions were finally moved into place – fourteen men sat down to a draughty dinner at the very top of what is still the world's tallest Corinthian column. Nelson himself was not present, his likeness only being winched up once the table and chairs had been cleared away.

Beneath the Thames: in September 1827 in a bid to show that his new Thames Tunnel at Wapping was perfectly safe Brunel organised an underwater banquet. The band of the Coldstream Guards was on hand to entertain 130 miners and 40 distinguished guests, but unfortunately the tunnel which had already claimed the lives of several workers collapsed again soon afterwards and the following January the waters of the Thames rushed back in once more.

Inside the stomach of a dinosaur: on New Year's Eve 1853 a dinner was held inside a partially completed iguanodon at Crystal Palace's celebrated Dinosaur Park. Hosted by Professor of Anatomy Richard Owen – based at the British Museum of National History he was the man who first coined the term dinosaur meaning 'terrible lizard' – the toast on the evening was as follows:

> Saurians and Pterodactyls all!
> Dream ye ever, in your ancient festivities,
> Of a race to come, dwelling above your tombs,
> Dining on your ghosts!

At the top of a power station chimney: as work continues to convert Battersea's famous Grade II-listed power station into a 38-acre living, leisure and lifestyle space, developers have unveiled plans which include a private dining room at the top of one of the popular icon's four towering 350ft chimneys.

Inside the Quadriga: on top of the Wellington Arch at Constitution Hill, Adrian Jones's gigantic winged figure of Peace standing in a chariot and pulling on the reins of four highly spirited stallions was the scene of a memorable dinner in 1912. The sculptor, a former officer in the Hussars, entertained seven guests to celebrate the conclusion of four years' work on his striking £17,000 bronze.

Above the Dome of St Paul's: although the great cathedral will always be Sir Christopher Wren's, a new cross and ball were installed by the Surveyor to the Fabric C.R. Cockerell in 1820 to replace the weatherbeaten originals. Once this had been done a small celebratory lunch was held inside the ball.

On the Metropolitan Line: During the First World War, despite licensing hours having been introduced at street level to keep munitions workers from drinking heavily, there were more than thirty underground bars on the tube network including buffets at Sloane Square and Liverpool Street. The last, Pat Mac's Drinking Den on the Metropolitan Line, didn't close until 1978.

DISHES AND DRINKS WITH LOCAL CONNECTIONS

The Sandwich: there is evidence suggesting something similar in the diet of the common Roman soldier, but tradition has it that the suggested insertion of a slice of meat between two of bread came from John Montagu, 4th Earl of Sandwich (1718–92). His family insist it was so he could continue working at his boxes at the Admiralty; it seems more likely that he was busy at the gaming table at White's.

Champagne: in 1662, having moved to London from Oxford, Christopher Merrett demonstrated how to make champagne at a meeting of the Royal Society – this a full thirty years before the more celebrated Dom Perignon accomplished it in France.

Maids of Honour: these puff-pastry cakes containing a rich melange of almonds, cinnamon, butter and brandy take their name from a famous terrace in Richmond. This was built for the ladies-in-waiting to a former Princess of Wales, Caroline of Anspach, who lived at nearby Richmond Palace.

Peach Melba: was created in 1893 at the Savoy by chef Auguste Escoffier to celebrate Dame Nellie Melba's visit to London. Combining the diva's favourites – peaches, raspberries, redcurrant jelly and vanilla ice cream – it did so in such way as to reduce the impact of cold ice cream on her priceless vocal cords. The dish made its debut at a dinner she was hosting, and was presented in an ice sculpture of a swan because she was currently appearing in *Lohengrin* at Covent Garden.

For Edward VII, Escoffier also created Cuisses de Nymphes a l'Aurore, the first time frogs' legs had ever appeared on an English menu.

Buck's Fizz: a mixture of champagne and orange juice is said to have been devised by a barman at Buck's Club called McGarry, although some authorities insist its origins pre-date the club which was founded by returning army officers only in 1919.

The Salisbury Steak: gone but not quite forgotten this late nineteenth-century chopped-beef patty was created by nutritionist Dr J. Salisbury. It was half-heartedly revived during the First World War as a patriotic substitute for the hamburger which to many sounded altogether too German.

John Collins: a lemon-flavoured bourbon- or Dutch gin-based cocktail devised by a barman of this name at Limmer's, a hotel at the corner of Hanover Square and Conduit Street which closed in 1817.

Chelsea Bun: until 1839 Chelsea in London was famous for its Bun House, with George II, III and IV all patronising its premises on the corner of Pimlico Road and Lower Sloane Street. The light fluffy buns contain raisins, and the genuine article is always square.

The RAC: the negative associations of drink and driving have more or less done for this gin and vermouth-based cocktail, created at the eponymous Pall Mall club by barman Fred Faecks in 1914.

Gin: the name is derived from a corruption of the old French, *genevre*, meaning juniper, but Londoners took to it in a big way as a result of some ill-advised laws introduced by William III to discourage the buying of imported spirits. By 1730 it was so cheap that one in seven houses in the East End were selling their own, and annual consumption in London doubled in less than a decade. Eventually the Gin Act got things under control, and the population returned to beer.

Steak & Kidney Pie: the Guinea Grill in Bruton Street, W1, sells more than 25,000 of them a year, their recipe having been officially declared Steak Pie of the Century in the millennium year.

LONDON TAVERNS WITH STRANGE TALES TO TELL

The Silver Cross (Whitehall, SW1) is unique among boozers as it is technically licensed as a brothel. No-one has seen fit to revoke the privilege granted it by Charles I, this despite the pub's close proximity to the House of Commons. Come to think of it, perhaps that's why no-one has. (The word boozer, incidentally, is a London coining too, being derived from a corruption of the Middle-English 'bousen' which is thieves' slang for drinking to excess.)

The Prospect of Whitby (Wapping Wall, E1) commands fantastic panoramic views across the Thames as well as affording visitors a glimpse of a more gruesome past. It is known to have been the haunt of river pirates who stole from corpses they dragged from the river, and the nearby Execution Dock is where Captain Kidd among many others was hanged. As was traditional with pirates and mutineers, his body was then left in a cage so the tide could wash over it three times.

The Mayflower (Rotherhithe Street, SE16) has for many years been granted a unique licence to sell both British and American postage stamps. This is thanks to its long ties with the former colony, the Pilgrim Fathers having set off from the pub's back steps in 1620.

The Hoop & Grapes (Aldgate High Street, EC3) is almost certainly the oldest pub in the capital, with origins dating back to the thirteenth century. Rumours persist of a tunnel (now blocked, of course) linking it to the Tower of London; it has also been suggested in this connection that the name Aldgate may be a corruption of 'ale gate', with visitors pausing here for refreshment on their way into the City.

Ye Olde Cheshire Cheese (Wine Office Court, EC4) is a replacement for the original building which was reduced to ashes in the Great Fire. Thus the cellars are much older, and incorporate part of the undercroft of a 600-year-old Carmelite monastery. In 1918 the tavern hit the headlines when the landlord's pet parrot fainted after mimicking the sound of 400 bottles of champagne popping open to mark the Armistice (see Chapter 10 for more).

The Magpie & Stump (Old Bailey, EC4) used until 1868 to charge extra for drinks taken upstairs where punters could enjoy an unrestricted grandstand view of the public hangings held across the street outside Newgate Gaol. Still a favourite watering hole for lawyers, one room here is traditionally known as Court No. 10, Nos 1 to 9 being across the road in the Central Criminal Court.

The Lamb & Flag (Rose Street, WC2) used to be called the Bucket of Blood. This was because its location, well hidden away up a narrow alleyway between two busy thoroughfares, made it an ideal venue for illegal prize fights. It is also where, in 1679, the Poet Laureate

Dryden was set upon and beaten after penning a few scurrilous lines about the Duchess of Portsmouth, Charles II's new mistress.

The Bride of Denmark (Queen Anne's Gate, SW1) is actually a private public house. In the 1940s architectural writer Hubert de Cronin started rescuing bits of pubs damaged in the blitz. The best – including a majestic stuffed lion in a glass case, a wealth of engraved and cut glass, carved wood and fine panelling – he installed in a warren of Victorian-style rooms beneath the offices of the Architectural Press as a private drinking club for staff members and their friends.

The Anglesea Arms (Selwood Terrace, SW7) lacks the grisly associations of the Krays' Blind Beggar in the Mile End Road but is nevertheless where Bruce Reynolds and a colleague met to discuss the feasibility of mounting what was to become the Great Train Robbery. The original plan was to steal a ton or more of gold arriving from South Africa; but in the end they had to settle for sacks and sacks of old banknotes and several years at Her Majesty's Pleasure.

LONDON PUB NAMES, & WHAT THEY MEAN

The Blue Posts (Bennet Street, SW1). Like an early cab rank, the posts in question – which have given their names to several pubs in central London – were traditionally where one went to pick up a sedan chair. The men who bore the load, the chairmen, are also commemorated in several pub names.

I Am the Only Running Footman (Charles Street, W1). Originally known as the Running Horse, what became the longest pub name in London, and the second longest in England, was coined in the 1770s by the 4th Duke of Queensbury in honour of a manservant who was said to be able to keep up a very respectable 8mph.

The John Snow (Broadwick Street, W1). Named not for the Channel Four News anchorman, but for the anaesthetics pioneer of the same name. Dr Snow (1813–58) also discovered that cholera was communicated by contaminated water, which is presumably why most people in the pub drink beer instead.

The Widow's Son (Devon Road, E3). Once a year a sailor hangs a hot-cross bun over the bar in a ritual stretching back more than two centuries. In so doing he commemorates a real widow who, expecting her son home for Easter, kept a warm bun for him. Sadly he never returned but each year until her death she added another bun to the moulding, blackened bundle which is preserved and honoured today by the pub regulars.

The Barrowboy & Banker (Borough High Street, SE1). Housed in a former bank, the name was supposed to commemorate the proximity of the nearby market and the City over the river and the contrasting types who work in each. Many who patronise the pub today, however, will have noticed that it is increasingly difficult to tell one from the other.

Cutty Sark (Ballast Quay, SE10). Named after the famous tea-clipper now stranded in dry dock nearby, the pub occasionally hosted the famous 'Whitebait Dinners'. From 1715 to 1894, with a few interruptions, these were annual banquets held on or near Trinity Sunday. Originally for workers involved in flood defences, they eventually became quite smart affairs attended by the PM and his Cabinet.

THE OLDEST RESTAURANTS IN TOWN

Rules (Maiden Lane, WC2). With an uninterrupted run and on the same site since 1798 Thomas Rule's establishment was first noted for 'porter, pies and oysters' – most of which are still on the menu today. Deeply traditional, although sadly London's oldest restaurant has abandoned a dress code in order to attract tourists, the premises were equipped with a special door so that Edward VII could enter unobserved when entertaining Lillie Langtry. Other Rules regulars included Dickens, H.G. Wells and Graham Greene.

Wilton's (Jermyn Street, SW1). Founded half a century earlier, but as a shellfish stall in the Haymarket, it received its first royal warrant as a purveyor of oysters to Queen Victoria in 1884. It nearly closed in 1942 when a German bomb landed on the nearby Wren church, the owner deciding she had finally had enough. Fortunately among her customers that day included banker Olaf Hambro who looked up from his oysters and asked for the restaurant to be added to his bill. His family still owns it today.

Simpsons-in-the-Strand (Strand, WC2). Originally the Grand Cigar Divan, a popular haunt of chess players, its origins can be traced to 1818 although the original premises were destroyed in order that the street could be widened. It was eventually rebuilt by T.E. Collcutt, who also built its parent the Savoy Hotel, and reopened in 1904.

The Café Royal (Regent Street, W1). Quite over the top with its rich, mirrored crimson and gold-gilt Rococo interior. While the exterior is wholly unremarkable, the grill room dates back to 1865 and looks much as it must have done when Oscar Wilde was a regular. A popular if bizarre boxing venue.

F. Cooke (Kingsland High Street, E8) provides the strongest possible contrast with all of the above, being a perfectly preserved and delightfully traditional eel-and-pie shop. Dating from 1910, its interior is completely unspoiled: stained-glass windows on the domed skylights, beautiful green and cream tiling, and elegant and understated Baroque revival plasterwork all painstakingly maintained by this fifth-generation family concern.

A BED FOR THE NIGHT

During the Second World War, underlining its pre-eminence, Claridge's in Brook Street was home to George II of Greece, Queen Wilhelmina of the Netherlands, King Haakon of Norway, King Peter of Yugoslavia, the Grand Duchess Charlotte of Luxembourg, Princess Alexandra of the Hellenes and the Prime Minister of Poland.

The first ever demonstration of four-wheel drive pioneer Harry Ferguson's famous little tractor was also held there, in the somewhat untesting environment of the hotel's Art Deco ballroom.

In 1955 the same room saw hundreds of ex-PoWs and escapees crowding in to celebrate the premiere of the film *Colditz Story*. With the centrepiece a giant picture of the forbidding German fortress, one of their number, Earl Haig, admitted the picture still made him feel depressed ten years on.

The founder of the delightfully clubby, countryhouse-style Browns Hotel between Dover and Albemarle Streets was Lord Byron's butler, James Brown.

From 1896 the Connaught in Carlos Place was called the Coburg, but like the royal family it changed its name during the First World War in order to avoid any anti-German sentiment.

A comparative newcomer, the Ritz, like the Paris original, is named after the great César Ritz although he never worked there. He was actually the first manager of the Savoy, where he employed the great Auguste Escoffier in the kitchens.

Such was the renown of the Savoy in the early days that for a while the house orchestra was led by Johann Strauss, and a dishwasher by the name of Guccio Gucci was so inspired by the quality of the guests that he returned home to Italy to found his eponymous luxury goods firm.

At the same time the Savoy owed much of its popularity among the rich to its early use of electric lighting. It also had an especially high ratio of bathrooms to bedrooms at a time when even the very well-heeled did not yet expect an en-suite. (In fact it had seventy in total compared to its nearest rival which had only four, and when the Dorchester had just one bathroom for forty bedrooms.)

Eventually dismissed from the Savoy for unprofessional conduct Ritz went on to establish the Carlton Hotel in the Haymarket in 1899. Before the First World War he employed Ho Chi Minh as a pastry chef before the latter returned to North Vietnam to lead the Communist Party. In the Second World War, however, the hotel was badly bombed, then demolished and replaced by New Zealand House.

Though far less grand, the Grosvenor in Victoria was one of the first hotels to have a lift, although initially this was referred to only as a 'rising room'.

The rebuilt Dorchester Hotel proved immensely popular during the war, pioneering the use of dried seaweed and granulated cork as soundproofing between the rooms but also (more significantly) reputedly bomb-proof steel-reinforced concrete construction.

With its subterranean Turkish Bath probably London's most luxurious air raid shelter, Eisenhower was encouraged to use the Dorchester as his London base while one Canadian diplomat described an evening as being on 'a luxury liner on which the remnants of London society have embarked in the midst of this storm'.

Beating the Beckhams by a good quarter of a century, when Richard Burton and Elizabeth Taylor had a party at the Dorchester to celebrate Burton's fiftieth birthday, the decorators used 200 yards of gold lamé to decorate the tables, with red and gold balloons being used to deck out the costermonger barrows on which the food was presented.

In Park Lane the Great Room of the Grosvenor House Hotel, for many years the largest public room in Europe, was a skating rink before being remodelled as a ballroom.

Although the Berkeley was completely rebuilt in the 1970s, the new building retained the Lutyens writing room from the original together with all the chandeliers, several marble fireplaces and even some light brackets. By contrast the four-star London Park Hotel south of the river was previously a doss-house for Lambeth down-and-outs.

The Duchess of Duke Street was based on Mrs Rosa Lewis who ran the Cavendish Hotel from 1904 until 1952. At the outbreak of the First World War she removed a portrait of the Kaiser to the servants' loo, hanging it upside down and insisting this was 'the only throne fit for old Willie'. She had earlier been immortalised in *Vile Bodies* by Evelyn Waugh, as Lottie Crump of Shepheard's.

For many years the only hotel in the City, the Great Eastern, had several unique features including two Masonic temples, its own railway sidings bringing in coal and taking away waste, and weekly deliveries of sea-water so that the guests could enjoy natural brine baths.

Staying at the Savoy, Marlene Dietrich always insisted she sleep in Claudio Buttafiva's bed, the hotel's reception manager at the time apparently having the largest bed on the premises.

9

LITERARY LONDON

POSTCODES WHERE NOTABLE WORKS WERE PENNED

EC1	*Paradise Lost*	John Milton in Bunhill Row, or Artillery Row as it was at the time (1662–74)
	Utopia	Thomas More at Crosby Place, Bishopsgate
EC3	*Troylus and Crysyede*	Geoffrey Chaucer at 2 Aldgate High Street
EC4	*The Dictionary*	Samuel Johnson, 17 Gough Square
	Fanny Hill:	John Cleland while
	Memoirs of a Woman	imprisoned for debt in the
	of Pleasure	Fleet just off Farringdon Street
N1	*The Traveller*	Oliver Goldsmith at Canonbury Tower, Canonbury Place
NW1	*Middlemarch*	Marian Evans (George Eliot) at 21 North Bank, Lodge Road
	Father and Son	Edmund Gosse at 17 Clarence Terrace
NW3	*Hadrian the VIIth*	Frederick Rolfe (Baron Corvo) at 69 Broadhurst Gardens
	Pamela, or Virtue Rewarded	Samuel Richardson at 40 North End Crescent
	The Forsyte Saga	John Galsworthy at Grove Lodge, Admiral's Walk
SE1	*Songs of Innocence and Experience*	William Blake at 13 Hercules Buildings, Hercules Road
SE5	*The Stones of Venice*	John Ruskin at 163 Denmark Hill
SE9	*The Railway Children*	E. Nesbit, Well Hall, Well Hall Road
SW1	*Cavalcade* and *This Happy Breed*	Noel Coward at 17 Gerald Road

SW1	*Rosamund*	Algernon Swinburne at 18 Grosvenor Place
	Almayer's Folly	Joseph Conrad at 17 Gillingham Street
	The Corsair	Lord Byron at 4 Bennet Street
SW3	*Importance of Being Ernest, Lady Windermere's Fan*, etc	Oscar Wilde at 34 Tite Street
	Peregrine Pickle	Tobias Smollet at 16 Lawrence Street
	Three Men in a Boat	Jerome K. Jerome, Chelsea Gardens
	Frederick the Great	Thomas Carlyle at 24 Cheyne Row
SW18	*The Mill on the Floss*	Marian Evans (George Eliot) at 31 Wimbledon Park Road.
W1	*For Services Rendered*	William Somerset Maugham at 6 Chesterfield Street
	Candida	George Bernard Shaw at 29 Fitzroy Square
	The Diary of a Nobody	George and Weedon Grossmith at 3 Spanish Place
	The Eustace Diamonds	Anthony Trollope at 39 Montagu Square
	The Rivals	Richard Brinsley Sheridan at 22 Orchard Street
W2	*Pastors and Masters*	Ivy Compton-Burnett at 59 Leinster Square
	Peter Pan	J.M. Barrie at 100 Bayswater Road
W6	*King Solomon's Mines*	H. Rider Haggard at 69 Gunterstone Road
	News from Nowhere	William Morris, 26 Upper Mall
W8	*The Wind in the Willows*	Kenneth Grahame at 16 Phillimore Place
	Vanity Fair	William Makepeace Thackeray at 16 Young Street
W11	*Down and Out in Paris and London*	George Orwell at 10 Portobello Road
WC1	*Bleak House, Little Dorrit*, etc	Charles Dickens at Tavistock House, Tavistock Square
	Queen Victoria	Lytton Strachey at 51 Gordon Square
	The Prisoner of Zenda	Anthony Hope (Sir Anthony Hope Hawkins) at 41 Bedford Square

	The Wind among the Reeds	W.B. Yeats, 18 Woburn Buildings
	Thesaurus	P.M. Roget at 18 Upper Bedford Place
WC2	*Erewhon*	Samuel Butler at Clifford's Inn, Fetter Lane
	Man and Superman and *Major Barbara*	George Bernard Shaw in his wife's flat at 10 Adelphi Terrace

ADDRESSES IMMORTALISED IN PRINT

221b Baker St, W1: When Conan Doyle installed his great detective at no. 221 the street numbering ran no further than 85. Eventually extended in 1930, the new 221 was eventually subsumed into the London headquarters of the Abbey National Building Society which for years continued to receive fan mail for the fictional detective.

110a Piccadilly, SW1: Another fictitious address for another great fictitious detective, Dorothy L. Sayer happened upon no. 110a for Lord Peter Wimsey's chambers, the insertion of the 'a' suggesting either an act of homage to Sherlock or a sly parody.

10 Rillington Place, W11: A place of such great infamy that following the John Christie murders (and Sir Ludovic Kennedy's tremendous book) it was renamed Rushton Close before being pulled down completely. Today part of Bartle Road occupies the site.

84 Charing Cross Road, WC2: Choosing this as the title of her enduring best-seller and popular play, Helene Hanff ensured that the address would be remembered long after the name of the bookseller – Marks & Co. – had been forgotten.

27a Wimpole Street: The enviable, book-lined chambers occupied by Professor Higgins in *My Fair Lady* are supposedly at this address, although in reality the premises are occupied by a doctors' surgery.

WORTH TRACKING DOWN:
21 RARE BOOKS ON LONDON

The Book of London, Roger Baker & Iain Macmillan, Michael Joseph, 1969

A City at Risk, Simon Jenkins, Hutchinson, 1970

The City, Jacques Lowe (Ed.) Quartet, 1982

Dockland, S.K. al Naib, GLC/North East London Polytechnic, 1986

An Encyclopaedia of London, William Kent, Dent, 1970

The Face of London, Harold P. Clunn, Spring Books, 1957

The Gentlemen's Clubs of London, Anthony Lejeune, Parkgate Books, 1997

Goodbye London, Christopher Booker & Candida Lycett-Green, Fontana, 1973

The Great Houses of London, David Pearce, Vendome Press, 1986

Inside the House of Lords, Clive Aslet & Derry Moore, HarperCollins, 1998

Leather Armchairs, Charles Graves, Cassell, 1963

Len Deighton's London Dossier, Jonathan Cape, 1967

The London Nobody Knows, Geoffrey Fletcher, Penguin, 1965

The London Rich, Peter Thorold, Viking, 1999

London Sight Unseen, Snowdon, Weidenfeld & Nicolson, 1999

London's Lost Riverscape, C. Ellmers & A. Werner, Viking, 1988

London's Pride, Mireille Galinou (Ed.), Anaya, 1990

Microcosm of London, T. Rowlandson & A.C. Pugin, King Penguin, 1947

Private Palaces, Christopher Simon Sykes, Chatto & Windus, 1985

The Rise of the Nouveaux Riches, J. Mordaunt Crook, John Murray, 1999

Tower of London, Christopher Hibbert, Newsweek, 1971

FILMS NAMED AFTER PARTS OF LONDON

Balham Gateway to the South
   (1971)
Les Bicyclettes de Belsize (1968)
A Nightingale Sang in Berkeley
   Square (1979)
The Bermondsey Kid (1933)
Imelda Marcos of Bethnal Green
   (2004)
The Britannia of Billingsgate
   (1933)
The Blackheath Poisonings (1992)
Tilly of Bloomsbury (1921)
Bond Street (1948)
84 Charing Cross Road (1987)
Chelsea Girls with Andy Warhol
   (1976)
Joe Brown at Clapham (1965)
The Courtneys of Curzon Street
   (1947)
Deptford Graffiti (1991)
The Girl from Downing Street
   (1918)
Duchess of Duke Street (1976)
East End Hustle (1976)
Greek Street (1930)
Greenwich Mean Time (1999)
The Lonely Lady from Grosvenor
   Square (1922)
Half Moon Street (1986)
The Foxes of Harrow (1945)
The Monster of Highgate Ponds
   (1961)

Hyde Park Corner (1935)
No. 5 John Street (1922)
The Kensington Mystery (1924)
The Lambeth Walk (1939)
The Lavender Hill Mob (1951)
It Happened in Leicester Square
   (1949)
A Murder in Limehouse (1919)
East of Ludgate Hill (1937)
Murder in Mayfair (1942)
Notting Hill (1999)
A Park Lane Scandal (1915)
Die Ballade von Peckham Rye
   (1966)
Piccadilly Playtime (1936)
Passport to Pimlico (1949)
Fly a Flag for Poplar (1974)
Horace of Putney (1923)
The Duchess of Seven Dials
   (1920)
Siege of Sidney Street (1960)
Emmanuelle in Soho (1981)
Soap Opera in Stockwell (1973)
The Stratford Adventure (1954)
Victoria (1995)
Waterloo Road (1945)
Mr Palfrey of Westminster (1984)
The Black Sheep of Whitehall
   (1941)
The Wimbledon Poisoner
   Wimbledon (1994)
Barretts of Wimpole Street (1956)

POP ACTS FAMILIAR FROM LONDON ROAD SIGNS

All Saints
Amen Corner
Angel
Bakerloo
Bethnal
Bo Street Runners
Bush
Chancery Lane
Chelsea
City
East 17
Eric Clapton
Gidea Park
Hatfield & The North
Highway
Inner Circle
Kensington Market
Kilburn & the Highroads
King's X
Lavender Hill Mob
Leyton Buzzards
London
Notting Hillbillies
Parliament
Parish Hall
Piccadilly Line
Real Westway
Road
Shaftesbury
Stamford Hillbillies
Strand
Towers of London
Townshend Lane
Wilderness Road

10

NATURAL HISTORY

The Ground beneath Your Feet

What we call the London Basin is a thick layer of clay, gravels and sand on a bed of chalk. The latter is the result of global warming and sea levels around the world rising up to flood much of the land. The area now occupied by London, for example, would otherwise have been a long way from dry land, the chalk bed being a massive accumulation of skeletons from literally trillions of tiny marine species. The clay, gravels and sand have resulted from the gradual weathering of the chalk over millions of years and desposits left on it by glaciers and rivers traversing the resulting plateau.

As for the basin shape – and from tall buildings such as those at Canary Wharf one can actually discern the shape – this was produced by the bedrock buckling as the continent of Africa piled into Europe. The admittedly rather more impressive Alps are a product of the same massive geological forces.

Notwithstanding the ongoing difficulties experienced by customers of Thames Water, the basin shape also gives the city its own natural fresh water supply. This arises because rain falling on the Chilterns or North Downs permeates the chalky ground and then runs down into the basin where it becomes trapped between the layers of impermeable clay. It's still there now, although with less heavy industry in the city than ever before what this actually means is that Londoners' rising water bills because of shortages combine with an increased risk of flooding.

Periods of global warming interspersed with occasional ice ages meant the flora and fauna of London were not always as they are

now. Excavations in Trafalgar Square, for example, have in the past uncovered the remains not just of feral pigeons but also of a hippopotamus, various elephants, bears, bison and deer, even of lions. Similarly in 1888 when a new artesian well was bored 400ft beneath Queensway in Bayswater the drilling crew recovered several sharks' teeth and other marine fossils.

DRESSING FOR AN ENGLISH SUMMER: LONDON WEATHER

The capital's first broadcast weather forecast went out on the BBC evening news bulletin on 14 November 1922 and the first weather map was shown on television, transmitted from Alexandra Palace, on 1 November 1936. The service was withdrawn in 1939, however, when all weather information was classified as secret because of the war with Germany. It didn't restart until 1947.

London's Camden Square has twice returned the highest maximum monthly temperatures ever recorded in Britain: for May (29.4°C in 1949) and June (35.6°C in 1957).

A freezing day being one where the daytime temperature never rises above 0°C, Kew recorded an astonishing nine freezing days in a row from 17–25 January 1963. Experts agree that this particular winter was in general as cold as the famous freeze of 1740 but not quite as cold as 1684, the coldest in UK 'instrumental' (i.e. recorded) history.

That same year, 1963, the river above Kingston-upon-Thames was covered with ice of sufficient thickness for locals to walk across it although further downstream waste heat from the power station prevented a similar build-up.

Central London's last true Frost Fair on the Thames, however, was in 1814. Ice floes drifted down from the upper reaches of the river and, becoming blocked by the narrow arches of the old London Bridge, coalesced into one lumpy mass. Stalls and entertainments were set up, and for five days much jollity was had. Unfortunately several lives were lost and many vessels wrecked when the thaw began in earnest.

On 6 January 1928 a depression moving down the North Sea caused a storm surge which travelled up the Thames, overwhelming the embankments and flooding the Tate Gallery to the top of the ground floor doors. Scores of paintings were destroyed, fourteen people were drowned and 4,000 Londoners made homeless.

On 1 July 1968 tens of thousands of cars in London were stained yellow when an estimated 5,000 tons of sand transported up from the Sahara by a slow southerly airflow were washed to the ground in a dramatic thunderstorm.

The foggiest year on record in London was 1873 when seventy-four days of thick fog were recorded. Six years later the worst single month for fog was December 1879, with seventeen days recorded.

On 14 August 1975 – the height of summer – 6.7in of rain fell on Hampstead in less than two and a half hours. Coming at the end of a three-week heatwave, it was almost certainly the worst such incident in more than a century: basements flooded; cars floated off down the road; two people were struck by lightning; and one man drowned.

Elsewhere on the same day many gardens in the area were reported to be under nearly a foot of hailstones, looking according to an article in the *Journal of Meteorology* like 'a sea of icy porridge'. The largest were measured and found to be ¾in in diameter.

On 16 August 1970 a huge lump of ice, a so-called hydro- or ice meteor, crashed through a conservatory roof in Isleworth. Five years later, on 25 January, a similar block weighing 48lb seriously damaged the roof of a house in Fulham. But even this was dwarfed by the 110lb monster which smashed into the bedroom of a house in Ponder's End on 2 January 1977.

The average start of the 'snow season', if London can be said to have such a thing, is the first week of December. In 1975, however, snow fell on Lord's Cricket Ground on 2 June.

A clerk at Cox & King's Bank in Waterloo Place for fifty years, Arthur Mackins (1908–90) proved adept at forecasting the weather in his spare time. Eschewing conventional measures he relied upon a variety of unorthodox phenomena including volcanic activity, comets, the temperature of the sea and even the shape of spiders' webs at home in his garden. He was, nevertheless, more often than not correct and as a consequence was frequently consulted by sports events organisers, nervous brides, and at least one leading ice-cream maker keen to meet demand with adequate supply.

A ROCK-HUNTERS GUIDE TO LONDON

The London Wall
With nothing but clay locally – good for bricks, but not much else – Londoners were forced from a very early date to import building stone. In fact this process has been ongoing from the earliest days, ever since the Romans, keen to build sturdy and enduring fortifications such as this one, started bringing rag or sandstone up the Medway and along the Thames from Kent.

The Tower of London
Built of pale Caen stone, the central White Tower was so named because it was originally whitewashed in order to further reinforce the visual effect of its dominating position (and that of the conquering Normans) over the surrounding city. Like England's new king the stone of choice came from Normandy, and was used in many of their other fortifications around the country.

St Mary Magdalene, East Ham
Still gloriously Norman except for its sixteenth-century tower and a small porch, and built using a huge variety of different material from many different sources. Here the familiar Caen stone and

Kentish ragstone are supplemented by chalk and flint from Purley in Surrey, Norfolk pudding-stone, and even reused Roman tiles.

The Albert Memorial
Literally a geologist's countrywide tour in miniature, the memorial includes pillars of pink granite from Ross and Mull, a base of grey Cornish granite, and numerous fossils in the paving stones which came from Hopton Wood, Derbyshire. Other paving material, the more orangey stuff, is from the Mansfield area and would once have formed sand dunes in an early British desert. The famous frieze is of Carrara marble from Italy, and if you look carefully you will also find fragments of exotic Blue John, a highly decorative form of fluorite from the Peak District.

The Economist Building
An award-winner when it first took shape in the architecturally conservative area of St James's Street in 1962–4, Alison and Peter Smithson's Economist Building (actually a group of three unequal-height towers) is another popular destination for fossil-hunters due to the high number of specimens visible in its Portland stone cladding.

Euston Station
The newest London terminus replacing what had until the 1960s been the oldest, Euston station's gleaming 647ft façade boasts among other things the largest volume of rare black Bushveld gabbro stone anywhere outside South Africa's Transvaal.

Victoria & Albert Museum
Inside the ornate main entrance of the Aston Webb building which replaced William Cubitt's 'Brompton Boilers', the columns are of Italian Breccia Violetta stone, the name meaning broken violet.

London Ismaili Centre
Providing an exotic counterpoint to conventional South Kensington this cultural centre cleverly advertises itself to the Muslim community through its use of two holy colours. The white effect is achieved by using pale grey granite, something which contrasts

strongly with the beautiful, iridiscent hue of its Brazilian blue bahia syenite detailing. Also known as sodalite, this was chosen in preference to the lapis lazuli the Aga Khan had agreed to fund (as leader of the Ismailis) because it was thought this would prove irresistable to thieves.

Natural History Museum

At last a clay building in London! Although even here in order to find clays of suitable quality to be moulded and cooked up into terracotta it was necessary to travel as far as Reading to locate the right material.

ANIMALS WITH UNUSUAL LONDON ASSOCIATIONS

Camberwell Beauty   A butterfly first seen in south-east London in 1748. In the 1920s it was portrayed in a giant mural of Doulton ceramic tiles (made in Lambeth and erected on the side of a library in Wells Way). This was hastily painted over when in one of his wartime broadcasts the Nazi Lord Haw-Haw said the Luftwaffe used it to navigate.

Cheshire Cheese Parrot   A long-time resident of this famous Fleet Street pub, the landlord's celebrated pet bird had a vocabulary so blue and so extensive that when it died at the age of forty in 1926 the BBC accorded it the unique honour of announcing its demise on the wireless.

Honey Bees   London's leading beekeeper, Clapham-based apiarist James Hamill has by his own reckoning in excess of 10,000,000 bees in 100 or so working hives stashed around south London. At least 25,000 of them come to work with him every day, beavering away in a unique glass-walled hive in his shop which sells anything and everything to do with the industrious little *Apis mellifera*. With such a wide variety of pollens available from small town gardens and window-boxes their honey is exceptional.

Guy the Gorilla   So named because he arrived at London Zoo on 5 November 1947, Guy proved to be one of the most popular residents until his death more than thirty years later. So popular, indeed, that he was later stuffed and mounted at the Natural

History Museum, and commemorated with a statue at the zoo and another in Crystal Palace.

Jumbo the Elephant   In 1255 Henry III was given an elephant by his cousin Louis IX and kept it at the Tower, but arriving in Regent's Park in 1865 the celebrated Jumbo was England's first African elephant and proved immensely popular. Unfortunately he grew wild and unreliable and despite public protests was sold to Barnum's Circus and shipped to the US where he was killed by a train. His name lives on, however, being applied to anything enormous: such as, for example, the £2,000 cheque handed over by Phineas T. Barnum.

Kaspar the Cat   Typical of the hotel which tries to think of everything, at the Savoy Hotel they keep a large figure of a cat which in the event of thirteen friends sitting down to eat is given its own table setting. This is done of course to allay any worries about bad luck arising from the proceedings, Kaspar himself having been created by the hotel interior designer Basil Ionides.

Mother Goose   Probably not a bird actually, although the absence of a Christian name is suspicious. Either way, the church registers at St Olave, Hart Street, EC3, record the death and burial on 14 September 1586 of a 'Mother Goose'.

Rats and Eels   Many thousands of eels are known to inhabit London's ancient sewers but their numbers are dwarfed by

between twelve and twenty million examples of *Rattus norvegicus*. The largest populations of these ferocious and alarmingly fertile brown rats, which arrived in London from Russia in the eighteenth century, are known to frequent Westminster where the higher than average proportion of cafés and restaurants guarantees them rich pickings.

Westminster Abbey Parrot   The effigy in the Abbey of Frances, Duchess of Richmond and Lennox – a rare, unrequited love of Charles II, who also modelled for 'Britannia' on the new pennies issued at the Restoration – is accompanied by a stuffed bird known to have lived with her for more than forty years. In fact the bird outlived its mistress, finally coming to join her here in 1702.

Dick Whittington's Cat   While not quite the equal of his pantomime alter ego, it's possible the four-times Lord Mayor of London kept a cat if only to keep the vermin under control. Certainly when the church of St Michael Paternoster Royal was restored (where Whittington funded the foundation) the mummified remains of a feline were discovered concealed within the fabric.

Cocky the Cockatoo   His name may have lacked a little imagination, but London Zoo's most popular and long-lived bird finally passed away in 1982 having been born when Queen Victoria was still on the throne.

HORSES FOR COURSES

With the car increasingly Public Enemy No. 1, and average speeds in the capital at around 8mph still no higher than they were a century ago, it's nevertheless a mistake to imagine that the streets of London would have been any more pleasant when horsepower meant exactly that.

By the end of the nineteenth century there were 250–300,000 working horses in the capital, each producing between 3 and 4 tons of dung a year, making a total in excess of a million tons of the stuff. London's flies had never had it so good, the smell must have been horrendous, and it's little wonder than typhoid and dysentery were rampant.

Horses were also involved in an average of 175 fatal accidents a year, fatal to humans that is, while their annual consumption of more than a million tons of food produced its own problems in terms of transport, storage and logistics.

Nevertheless, they had a good run. Working the Old Kent Road the last horse-tram was finally taken out of service in 1913, the last horse-bus three years later, and the last horse-carriage for hire only disappeared in 1920. Even then, by 1935, there were still 20,000 horse-drawn carts on the capital's arterial roads – making up 5% of the total – and the last horse-drawn cab wasn't finally retired until 1947.

Horses were also a danger to themselves, frequently slipping on wet cobbles and metalled roads so that every London rail terminus had to have its own horse 'ambulance' to cope with disaster. (1,300 horses were employed in the environs of King's Cross alone.) There were also several horse hospitals to patch them up again, such as the one which now forms part of Camden Market.

One finds evidence of London's equine past in several street names too. Horseferry Road commemorates a sixteenth-century ferry which took men and animals across the Thames until 1750 when the first Lambeth Bridge was built. Similarly Horseleydown Lane is a corruption of Horsey Down and refers to a 5-acre pasture owned by Bermondsey Abbey and used for grazing.

The current equine population of London is hard to gauge – urban livery stables are prohibitively expensive, although the police and cavalry of course make their own arrangements – but Horseman's Sunday, the third in September, still sees a mounted service for those who qualify. It takes place at the church of St John's – the one in Hyde Park Crescent, that is, not the altogether more appropriate-sounding one at Mare Street, Hackney.

Their legacy lives on elsewhere too, of course. For example in the fact that even the fastest and most advanced forms of the internal combustion engine, such as those used in modern Formula One cars, are still rated in terms of horsepower.

IT'S A DOG'S LIFE IN LONDON

An estimated 700,000 dogs live in the capital, approximately 10,000 of them passing through Battersea Dogs' Home each year. (And by the way it's not true that any dog not 'homed' within a week is destroyed. Happily this fate is reserved for those that are seriously ill or clearly dangerous.)

In Carlton House Terrace London's only authentic Nazi monument is a headstone marking the grave of the German Ambassador's dog Giro, which was accidentally electrocuted in February 1934.

In 1870 a bull-mastiff called Chance joined the brigade at Chandos Street Fire Station and proved himself adept at locating people in burning buildings. Unfortunately the heroic canine was killed by a collapsing wall in 1882, while attending a 'shout' at a printing works.

Using yellow lines of a different kind, Camden was the first local authority to paint the outline of a squatting dog on its pavements, together with with an arrow reminding owners to get their dogs to use the gutter.

In a similar move Islington Council once produced a slightly controversial anti-dog mess advertisement which featured a pyjama-clad resident 'doing his business' on the street.

In Victoria Park, east London, are two stone sentinel dogs, called the Dogs of Aleibiades. They were presented to the park in 1912 by Lady Regnant.

Thomas Carlyle's faithful mutt Nero is buried in the garden of his home at 24 Cheyne Row, Chelsea, and so now comes under the care of the National Trust.

Dogs travel free on the tube, the train and the bus; but they are allowed on buses only at the discretion of the driver and must sit upstairs.

Behind Kenwood House in north London are woods containing two headstones marking the graves of two hounds called Bill and Mac. Owned by Grand Duke Michael of Russia, second cousin to the last Tsar Nicholas II, they lived here when their master leased Kenwood from the 6th Earl of Mansfield from 1910 to 1917.

The name of the Isle of Dogs has never been satisfactorily explained, although the most likely answer is that royal hunstmen crossed the river from Greenwich to hunt in the marshes here. The name may have been bestowed on it by sailors on the Thames who during Henry VIII's reign could hear the animals baying for blood.

More than 200 pets are buried in the north-east corner of Kensington Gardens (behind Victoria Lodge). Their memorials date back to 1880 when a dog belonging to the Duke of Cambridge was run over nearby, since when the dog has been joined by numerous birds, cats and monkeys.

The Metropolitan Police has approximately 370 dogs on the force.

CATCHING LONDON ON THE WING

An incredible total of 357 different species of bird have been seen in the wild in London. Of these, however, many are rare visitors, the following 115 being exceptionally so having been logged by birdwatchers fewer than 25 times in the last hundred years.

Pied-billed Grebe
Little Shearwater
Mediterranean
  Shearwater
Storm Petrel
Little Bittern
Black-crowned Night
  Heron
Squacco Heron
Cattle Egret
Great White Egret
Purple Heron
Black Stork
White Stork
Glossy Ibis
Spoonbill
American Wigeon
Blue-winged Teal
Green-winged Teal
Ring-necked Duck
Lesser Scaup
Black Kite
White-tailed Eagle
Montagu's Harrier
Goshawk
Rough-legged Buzzard
Lesser Kestrel
Red-footed Falcon
Gyrfalcon
Crane
Black-winged Stilt
Collared Pratincole
Killdeer
Kentish Plover
Dotterel
American Golden Plover
Sociable Plover
Baird's Sandpiper
Broad-billed Sandpiper

Buff-breasted Sandpiper
Sharp-tailed Sandpiper
Solitary Sandpiper
Spotted Sandpiper
Western Sandpiper
White-rumped Sandpiper
Great Snipe
Long-billed Dowitcher
Marsh Sandpiper
Lesser Yellowlegs
Red-necked Phalarope
Wilson's Phalarope
Pomarine Skua
Great Skua
Long-tailed Skua
Bonaparte's Gull
Franklin's Gull
Ring-billed Gull
Bridled Tern
Caspian Tern
Gull-billed Tern
Roseate Tern
Sooty Tern
Whiskered Tern
Razorbill
Pallas's Sandgrouse
Yellow-billed Cuckoo
Snowy Owl
Common Nighthawk
Alpine Swift
Bee-eater
Roller
Crested Lark
Shore Lark
Short-toed Lark
Red-rumped Swallow
Olive-backed Pipit
Red-throated Pipit
Richard's Pipit

Tawny Pipit
Citrine Wagtail
Dipper
Bluethroat
Desert Wheatear
Grey-cheeked Thrush
Dusky Thrush
Aquatic Warbler
Barred Warbler
Blyth's Reed Warbler
Hume's Leaf Warbler
Icterine Warbler
Melodious Warbler
Paddyfield Warbler
Pallas's Warbler
Radde's Warbler
Sardinian Warbler
Savi's Warbler
Sub-alpine Warbler
Yellow-browed Warbler
Iberian Chiffchaff
Red-breasted Flycatcher
Short-toed Treecreeper
Crested Tit
Penduline Tit
Isabelline Shrike
Lesser Grey Shrike
Woodchat Shrike
Nutcracker
Raven
Rose-coloured Starling
Serin
Arctic Redpoll
Common Rosefinch
Black-headed Bunting
Little Bunting
Ortolan Bunting
Pine Bunting
Rustic Bunting

FLORA LONDINIUM

London Rocket or *Sysimbrium irio* is a plant which, hitherto native to countries bordering the Mediterranean, suddenly appeared (and in great profusion) in the areas of the City which had been devastated by the Great Fire.

Britain's tallest outdoor olive tree at more than 30ft is in Chelsea Physic Garden, this particular *Olea europaea* producing in one year (1976) a record 7lb of fruit. The same famous establishment also used to be home to London's only legitimate cannabis crop, but unfortunately – if somewhat predictably – once news about it got around it was 'harvested' one night by a scrumper or scrumpers unknown who bunked over the wall.

A mulberry tree still standing in the south-west corner of the gardens at Buckingham Palace is thought to be the one survivor of the 4 acres planted by James I in the hope of establishing an indigenous silk industry.

On 19 May every year – and the same silent but touching ritual has now been enacted for something approaching two centuries – a florist visits the church of St Peter ad Vincula on Tower Green in order to place a dozen red roses on Anne Boleyn's grave. Who pays for them has never been revealed, although a favourite candidate is a representative of the Duke of Northumberland's family, one of whose forebears was ousted in her affections by the feckless Henry VIII.

In another rose-related ceremony, a single bloom (also blood-red) is presented to the Lord Mayor of London each 24 June by the churchwardens of All-Hallows-by-the-Tower. Carried on a velvet cushion with considerable pomp it is the agreed fine or quit-rent due each year on an illegal construction dating back to 1381. That was the year Sir Robert Knollys built an unauthorised bridge from one of his properties in Seething Lane to another on the opposite side.

Known as the Old Lions, the oldest known trees at the Royal Botanical Gardens in Kew date back to 1762 and are the Maidenhair tree *Ginkgo biloba*, a Pagoda tree *Sophora japonica*, and an Oriental Plane *Platanus orientalis*. Together with examples of *Robinia pseudoacacia* and the *Zelkova carpinifolia*, they came from the Twickenham estate of the Duke of Argyll and were presented by Lord Bute, the Duke's nephew, who was botanical adviser to Princess Augusta.

Something of a giant panda of the plant world, Kew's cycad plant (*Encephalartos ferox*) has reportedly had so much trouble getting pollinated in the past that the staff responsible for its welfare now help it along using a turkey-baster. (Cycads apparently thrived during the Jurassic Period, 206 million years ago, but are perhaps unsurprisingly now threatened with extinction.)

With its own examples dating back to the sixteenth century, the collections of the Botany Department at the Natural History Museum in South Kensington comprise an incredible 5.2 million preserved specimens of every kind of plant. Including algae, diatoms, seaweeds, lichens, mosses, ferns, herbs, conifers and flowering species, and collected by the likes of Hans Sloane, Joseph Banks and Charles Darwin, a mere 10% are native species and approximately 1% can now be viewed on-line.

The strangest is perhaps the fabled 'Vegetable Lamb of Tartar', a prized specimen from Sir Hans Sloane's Vegetable Substances Collection. A popular feature of some illustrated medieval bestiaries, where it appears to suggest that sheep do actually grow on trees, in reality it is a type of fern rhizome which looks vaguely lamb-like, having the remnants of stalks for legs and fluffy golden wool on its outer surface.

The popular idea that the beginning of hostilities in the Wars of the Roses was marked by rivals from the houses of Lancaster and York plucking roses in London's Temple Gardens was sadly only ever a creation of William Shakespeare. Nevertheless red and white roses are still grown in the gardens by way of commemorating this now famous if fictional scene.

In 2006 a Putney man with some particularly well-stocked greenhouses in his back garden – and what the press referred to as a bad attack of orchidelirium – was gaoled after smuggling more than 100 rare plant species into Heathrow. Indeed one of the orchids in the haul, *Paphiopedilum gigantifolium*, is so rare that an expert at Kew admitted never having seen it before. (Only discovered in 1997 in Sulawesi, it had already become extinct in the wild nine years later.)

11

THE THAMES & ITS TRIBUTARIES

FATHER THAMES & THE LONDON REACHES

Almost certainly the second oldest geographical name in the country – only 'Kent' is known to beat it – Caesar called England's principal river the Tamesis, although the reason for this is no longer known.

The Thames did not always flow through London. A relatively young feature of the local landscape, until about half a million years ago it flowed from the Midlands through Oxfordshire before turning north-eastwards through Hertfordshire and East Anglia where it entered the sea at Ipswich. It only flowed down to what was to become London when a vast ice sheet reached England from Scandinavia thereby blocking its existing course – although that said, of course, had it not done so there would have been no London.

Until 1750 there was only one bridging point in London, and from 1197 until 1857 the Corporation of the City of London exercised its jurisdiction over the whole river from the mouth of the Medway through to Staines. After that date a very long row over ownership of the river bed was eventually settled in favour of Queen Victoria and the Crown.

No-one in his right mind would consider drinking from the Thames, but in fact when one drinks a glass of London tap water it has typically already passed through nine other people.

The Thames and its estuary are divided into reaches, although few Londoners are aware of their historic names or which is which.

Their often quite evocative names and extents are as follows, starting from Yantlet Creek:

Sea Reach	to West Blyth Buoy
Lower Hope	to Coalhouse Point
Gravesend	to Tilburyness
Northfleet Hope	to Broadness
St Clement's	to Stoneness
Long	to Dartford Creek
Erith Rands	to Coalharbour Point
Erith	to Jenningtree Point
Halfway	to Crossness
Barking	to Tripcock Point
Gallions	to Woolwich Hoba Wharf
Woolwich	to Lyle Park
Bugsby's	to Blackwall Point
Blackwall	to Dudgeon's Dock
Greenwich	to Deptford Creek
Limehouse	to Limekiln Creek
Lower Pool	to Cherry Garden Pier
Upper Pool	to London Bridge
[no name]	to Westminster Bridge
[no name]	to Vauxhall Bridge
Nine Elms	to Chelsea Bridge
Chelsea	to Battersea Bridge
Battersea	to Wandsworth Bridge
Wandsworth	to Putney Bridge
Barn Elms	to Hammersmith Bridge
Chiswick	to Chiswick Ferry
Corney	to Barnes Railway Bridge
Mortlake	to Kew Bridge

BAZALGETTE'S GREAT EMBANKMENT

London's great sewer guru Sir Joseph Bazalgette (1819–91) was, like his friends the Brunels, of French extraction although the origins of his extraordinary name are as obscure in France as they are here.

While he is known for helping brilliantly to alleviate the 'Great Stink' his largest single work was actually the Victoria Embankment.

This added an incredible 37 acres of new land to central London by reclaiming it from what had been described as a 'worthless foreshore where dead dogs and cats did mostly congregate'. By doing so of course he also rendered the name of the Strand somewhat meaningless.

Sneakily Prime Minister Gladstone attempted to claim all 37 acres for the Crown, hoping to cover them in offices in order to raise sufficient rental revenues to cancel the 'temporary' income tax William Pitt had introduced to fund the Napoleonic Wars.

Bazalgette had other things in mind for the land, however, including making room for five key amenities. These were:

His main sewer which runs from Hammersmith to West Ham.
A wide, tree-lined avenue which now, sadly, is the congested and rather unlovely A3211.
Embankment Gardens, a much needed 'green lung' in this part of the capital.
Somewhere beneath which could be run one of these new-fangled underground railways.
And finally a narrower service tunnel to accommodate water, gas and – eventually – electricity ducts beneath all of the above.

The public supported Bazalgette against the Prime Minister; so too did W.H. Smith (1825–91) whose efforts eventually won the day. These days remembered as a newsagent – the first branch was on the Strand – Smith was also a Member of Parliament, First Lord of the Admiralty and first Lord of the Treasury. In recognition of his achievements, his widow was raised to the ermine as Viscountess Hambleden.

Shipwrecks in the Thames

In the modern city of high-rise offices and seemingly endless redevelopment it's easy to forget its maritime past even with such names as Puddle Dock, Broken Wharf and Oystergate Walk still there to remind us. Nor, with literally centuries of trading on the river, should one be surprised that the Thames has thrown up so many significant shipwrecks over the years. With the remains of several now in the Museum of London, these provide a fascinating insight into a city which has been trading internationally for nearly 2,000 years.

In 1962 a large Romano-Celtic vessel was uncovered at Blackfriars. Archaeologists estimate it to have been 60ft long, with a beam of 20ft and a 40ft mast. An infestation of the salt-resistant common shipworm *Teredo navalis* shows that it must also have spent time at sea.

Believed to have sunk around AD 150, this particular vessel was carrying a cargo of building stone quarried from a site near Maidstone when the load – possibly as much as 50 tons of ragstone, one of an estimated 13,000 similar loads clearly destined for building the city walls – shifted, causing the ship to collide and sink.

Excavations at an old Roman quay close to Guys Hospital uncovered another barge-like vessel. 52ft long and 14ft wide, it is estimated to have had a maximum payload of 6 tons.

Among the cargo of another wreck found at Blackfriars, a clinker-built boat dated to about 1670, were 500 bricks which were probably being imported to rebuild the City after the Great Fire. Apparently a lighter, used for unloading larger sea-going vessels which stayed midstream, fragments of low-quality sea-coal were also found between its ribs suggesting it had been used to unload a collier travelling down from Newcastle.

In 1970 yet another ruined vessel was found at Blackfriars, probably the most complete medieval-period barge of its kind anywhere in Europe. Known as a shout, dendrochronological or tree-ring studies suggest a construction date of between 1380 and 1415, while the sinking has been put at about 1490 after an examination of the pottery cargo on board. Capable of carrying 7.5 tons of cargo, such a vessel could have been built in just three weeks by a team of four or five medieval craftsmen.

The 'reverse-clinker' construction of another small vessel, dated to 1570, has also prompted marine archaeologists to suggest that they have discovered at last a so-called London dungboat. Apparently by having the lower planks overlapping the upper ones (instead of the other, more conventional way) the grim task of unloading would have been made slightly easier.

Perhaps the most splendid discovery, however, was that made at 1912 during excavations further downriver at the Woolwich Power Station. Here the discovery of the bottom of an enormous ship with fine carvel planking has led historians to believe that this is none other than the remains of Henry VII's well-armed *Sovereign*. Sadly no contemporary pictures of the great warship remain, but by 1521 it had reportedly been abandoned in a decaying state in the dock at Woolwich.

ROWING THE RIVER

Full-scale races were a luxury rarely possible on a crowded, working river but on 18 May 1661 Samuel Pepys records finding 'the Thames full of boats and gallys, and upon inquiry found that there was a wager to be run this morning . . . but upon the start the wager boats fell foul one of another, till at last one of them gives over, pretending foul play, and so the other row away alone, and all our sport lost'.

The oldest such event in the world, the race known as Doggett's Coat and Badge, was conceived to mark and celebrate the anniversary of George I's accession to the throne. Comedian Thomas Doggett suggested a race between oarsmen between London Bridge and Chelsea Bridge, and it has been held that way each summer since 1715. Supervised by the Fishmongers' Company, and with only young members of the Worshipful Company of Watermen being eligible, the winner is presented with a scarlet coat and a large silver badge.

Only a relative newcomer, the University Boat Race from Putney to Mortlake has drawn crews from Oxford and Cambridge every March since 1829. The first Oxford crew included a bishop-to-be and the future deans of both Lincoln and Repton, while Cambridge responded with two bishops of its own, one dean-to-be and the future Chancellor of the Diocese of Manchester. Even now an estimated 30% of all rowing blues, from both universities, have been Old Etonians.

The first international race on the Thames took place on 17 August 1869 – a crew from Oxford convincingly beat Harvard – and since 1988 the Great River Race has taken place on the first Sunday in September. Fully handicapped to ensure fair play, this sees up to 200 traditional boats racing 22 miles from Richmond to the Isle of Dogs, everything from Chinese dragonboats to Viking longboats, Norwegian scows to Canadian canoes. Their crews compete for the Challenge Trophy of the Company of Watermen & Lightermen, coincidentally featuring a mounted Doggett badge originally issued to Gravesend oarsman William Savage in 1803.

LONDON'S LOST RIVERS: WHERE ARE THEY NOW?

As an expanding London encroached on the surrounding countryside it was the fate of many pretty rivers to degrade into sewers, open at first and later enclosed so that today little if any physical evidence of their existence remains at surface level.

The Neckinger takes its name from a neckinger or handkerchief, 'devil's neckinger' being London slang for the hangman's noose. The river itself rose in St George's Field near the Imperial War Museum, where it was also known as the Lock Stream. Passing close to the Elephant and Castle (where there was once a Lock Hospital) it flowed through the grounds of Bermondsey Abbey and entered the Thames at what is now St Saviour's Dock near the Design Museum.

The Earl's Sluice, since 1820 the Earl Main Sewer, rises near Denmark Hill and flows into the Thames at Rotherhithe after joining the River Peck. (This rises in Peckham Rye, hence the name.) Where it crosses the Old Kent Road there used to be a ford which would have been known to the Canterbury pilgirms; called Thomas-a-Watering, it was named after Thomas-a-Becket.

The Effra commences its journey towards the Thames in Upper Norwood, flowing through Dulwich – it could be seen in the grounds of Belair House – then Brockwell Park and into Brixton. From there it passes beneath St Mark's, the Commissioners' church in Kennington where the threat of the river flooding prevented a deep level shelter being built during the war, to curve beneath the Oval. It joins the Thames at Vauxhall, a far cry indeed from the Celtic *yfrid* or 'torrent' from which it takes its name.

The Fleet has its origins in the famous bathing ponds on Hampstead Heath, the river running down where Fleet Road is today, beneath the Regent's Canal, and on to King's Cross. Still navigable to Holborn in the eighteenth century, it was associated with a famous spa at Bagnigge Wells (patronised by Nell Gwynn who had a summer residence nearby). The name Clerkenwell also has a connection to this river, the actual 'clerks' well' having been rediscovered in 1924 beneath 16 Farringdon Lane. Unfortunately the proximity of livestock at Smithfield Market, with all that this suggests, quickly compromised the purity of its water, and the river, now just another sewer, continues on its way to join the Thames at Blackfriar's Bridge.

The Grand Surrey Canal was conceived as the only major canal south of the Thames, intended to run from the Surrey Docks through Camberwell and on to Mitcham with a link to Croydon. In the event this plan proved far too ambitious, and it reached no further than Peckham with a working life of less than thirty years. Converted to wharves in 1836, it closed in 1971 and was promptly filled in.

The Tyburn or Kings Scholar's Pond rises in Haverstock Hill and according to some authorities supplies the lake in Regents Park. Thereafter it flows into the old village of Marylebone (Mary-le-bourne, or burn) where it was, for example, observed flowing through a bomb crater near Wigmore Street during the Blitz. Avery Row in Mayfair is also known to have been built over the newly culverted river, and Shepherd Market would once have been held on one of its banks. Today the river, confined to a brick-lined tunnel, continues beneath Buckingham Palace and its outflow into the Thames can be seen from the south bank beneath Tyburn Cottage, an expensive white house on Grosvenor Road.

The Westbourne or 'west stream' is formed by the coming together of several streams west of Hampstead, and at one time was developed into the popular if short-lived Kilburn Spa. From there it flowed into Maida Vale, to Bayswater (this name a contraction from an associated spring called 'Bayard's Watering') across Westbourne

Terrace and into Hyde Park. Here the end of the Serpentine known as the Long Water was created by damming the Westbourne in 1730. More recently, however, the river has been diverted into Ranelagh Sewer and continues towards and beyond Sloane Square. It has twin outfalls into the Thames, positioned either side of Chelsea Bridge.

The Walbrook entered the ancient city by All Hallows London Wall and from Roman to medieval times was the chief watercourse for the city. These days though it is better known as the London Bridge Sewer and, performing only the function thus suggested, it runs approximately 35ft underground to meet the Thames just west of Cannon Street station. Skulls found in the river, and now in the Museum of London, are held to be victims of Queen Boudicca's assault on the Roman city.

BRIDGES OVER THE THAMES

Tower Bridge	1886-94	
London	1st century AD	Wooden bridge built
	1176–1209	Replaced with a stone one
	1762–1822	Altered substantially
	1823–31	Second stone one replaced
	1902–4	Widened
	1967	Sold to Americans
	1967–72	Existing bridge completed
Alexandra	1863–6	Railway into Cannon Street
Southwark	1814–19	
	1919–21	Replaced
Millennium	1998–2000	Pedestrian
Blackfriars Rail	1862–4	into Ludgate Hill
	1885	Demolished (piers remain)
	1884–6	Railway into Blackfriars
Blackfriars Road	1760–9	
	1860–9	Replaced
	1907–10	Widened
Waterloo	1811–17	
	1937–42	Replaced
Hungerford	1814–45	Pedestrians only
	1860–4	Rebuilt for railway
	1900	Widened
Hungerford Foot	2002	
Westminster	1738–50	
	1854–62	Replaced
Lambeth	1861–2	
	1929–32	Replaced

Vauxhall	1811–16	
	1895–1906	Replaced
Grosvenor	1858–60	Railway into Victoria
	1865/1907	Widened
	1963–7	Replaced
Chelsea	1851–8	
	1936–7	Replaced
Albert	1871–3	
	1884	Strengthened
	1971–3	New piers added
Battersea	1771–2	Footbridge (now demolished)
Battersea Rail	1861–3	
Battersea Road	1886–90	
Wandsworth	1870–3	
	1936–40	Replaced
Putney Rail	1887–9	
Putney Road	1727–9	
	1871–2	Altered substantially
	1973–6	Strengthened
Hammersmith	1824–7	Possibly just a footbridge
	1883–7	Existing bridge installed
	1973–6	Strengthened
Barnes	1846–9	Rail and pedestrians
	1891–5	Altered substantially
Chiswick	1933	
Kew Rail	1864–9	
Kew Road	1757	Wooden bridge
	1784–9	Stone bridge
	1903	Rebuilt
Richmond Lock	1894	Footbridge only
Twickenham	1931–3	
Richmond Rail	1848	
	1906–8	Altered substantially
Richmond Road	1774–7	
	1937–9	Widened
Teddington	1888–9	Footbridge only
Kingston Rail	1860–3	
	1907	Replaced
Kingston Road	*c.* 1219	Medieval bridge on record
	1376	Medieval bridge 'broken down'
	c. 1520	Medieval bridge repaired
	1825–8	Existing bridge completed
	1914	Widened
Hampton Court	1751–3	Bridge recorded
	1778	Rebuilt
	1865	Iron replacement
	1930–3	Replaced with existing bridge

TUNNELS UNDER THE THAMES

Compared to Paris, London has far fewer bridges over its principal river but more tunnels under water than it or any other city in the world. Several of those railway tunnels listed below, for example, are twins, making a total of twenty-three in all.

Woolwich	1876	Pedestrian only
Blackwall	1891–7	Northbound
	1960–7	Southbound
Greenwich	1897–1902	Pedestrian only
Rotherhithe	1904–8	
Thames	1805–43	Pedestrian
	1866–9	Rebuilt to take railway
	1884	Joins Metropolitan Line
Tower Subway	1869–70	Cable cars, then pedestrian only
Northern Line	1900	City Branch
City & South London	1890	First railway tunnel under river
Waterloo & City	1899	aka 'The Drain'
BT Cable	1950s	Waterloo to Queen Victoria Street
Bakerloo Line	1906	
BT Cable	1950s	Waterloo to Trafalgar Square
Northern Line	1926	West End Branch
Victoria Line	1968–71	
Battersea I	1937	Cables from power station
Battersea II	1937	Hot water to Dolphin Square
Thames Water	1860	Barnes Water Main

POLICING THE RIVER

It's estimated that by the eighteenth century at least £500,000-worth of goods were being pilfered annually from vessels moored on the Thames. In part this was because congestion on the river meant thousands of ships at a time were having to queue for several weeks before being able to dock or depart.

At today's prices that is equivalent to a loss of around £30 to £35 million, almost one-third of which was suffered by the Honourable East India Company. Many other companies lost half their cargo before it left the docks, the authorities acknowledging that one out of every three dockworkers at the time was a thief or receiver and as many as 100,000 Londoners similarly crooked.

The resulting scandal prompted magistrates Patrick Colquhoun and John Harriot to found the Marine Police Force in 1798, a full thirty-one years before London's regular police force was in operation.

The original force force comprised Harriot himself, a Chief Constable, a clerk and 200 men (100 armed), all paid for by the government. At the same time the West India Company employed its own watchmen on the quayside and built a moat and 30ft high wall around its docks, but still insisted its nearly 1,000 dockers wore a specially designed uniform in which stolen goods could not easily be concealed.

Today the River Police are based at Wapping, appropriately close to Execution Dock, the usual spot (in the words of John Stow in 1598) 'for the hanging of pirates and sea-rovers, at the low watermark and there to remain until three tides had overflowed them'. There is a museum on the same site, and at Garford Street some original Ships' Constables' cottages have been preserved.

With a fleet of twenty boats – fifteen patrol boats, a command vessel called the *Patrick Colquhoun*, and four rigid inflatables – the modern force is responsible for patrolling between Hampton Court and Dartford. Today the 89 officers or 'wet-bobs' are more likely to be involved in counter-terrorism measures – or pulling corpses from the water at a rate of 80–100 per year – than attempting to prevent piracy.

Any bodies which are recovered from the Thames, sometimes after twenty days in the water, are held at Wapping before being sent to the Coroner. (The stainless steel tub used for this purpose is concealed beneath a four-poster frame covered with blue tarpaulin which can be glimpsed from the river at Wapping.)

The River Police played a major role in the *Marchioness* disaster when fifty-one partygoers were drowned in 1989; also in the 1878 *Princess Alice* tragedy which claimed many many more. A paddleboat operated by the London Steamship Company, the *Alice* was struck by a collier called the *Bywell Castle* and nearly cut in half. She sank in less than five minutes, with the loss of approximately 640 lives including that of

Captain W. Grinstead of the *Alice* who was subsequently declared responsible for the worst disaster in inland British waters.

ISLANDS IN THE THAMES

Isle of Sheppey
Canvey Island
Lower Horse Island
Two Tree Island
Isle of Grain
Frog Island
Chiswick Eyot
Oliver's Island
Brentford Ait
Lot's Ait
Isleworth Ait
Corporation Island
Glover's Island
Eel Pie Island
Swan Island
Trowlock Island
Steven's Eyot
Raven's Ait
Boyle Farm Island
Thames Ditton Island
Ash Island
Tagg's Island
Garrick's Ait
Platt's Eyot
Sunbury Court Island
Swan's Rest Island
Rivermead Island
Sunbury Lock Ait
Wheatley's Ait
Desborough Island
D'Oyly Carte Island
Lock Island
Hamhaugh Island

Pharaoh's Island
Dumsey Eyot
Penton Hook Island
Truss's Island
Church Island
Hollyhock Island
Holm Island
The Island, Hythe End
Magna Carta Island
Pats Croft Eyot
Ham Island
Nickcroft Ait
Sumptermead Ait
Romney Island
Cutlers Ait
Firework Ait
Deadwater Ait
Baths Island
Queens Eyot
Monkey Island
Pigeonhill Eyot
Headpile Eyot
Bridge Eyot
Grass Eyot
Ray Mill Island
Boulters Island
Glen Island
Sonning Eye
View Island
De Bohun Island
Fry's or De Montfort Island
Pipers Island

12

ON THIS DAY IN LONDON

1 January 1967
George Harrison, though recognised by the doorman as a Beatle, was barred from Annabel's in Berkeley Square because he wasn't wearing a tie. He went to a Lyons Corner House instead, and celebrated the New Year there.

3 January 1963
John Hampden Hobart-Hampden-Mercer-Henderson, the 8th Earl of Buckinghamshire died and his title passed to someone called Fred who worked as a gardener for Southend Council and earned £9 a week.

4 January 1992
North London giants and FA Cup favourites Arsenal were unexpectedly knocked out of the running by fourth division Wrexham.

8 January 1938
A German tourist called Willie Hitler left the country after telling Fleet Street reporters that his uncle Adolf was actually a peaceful man 'who thinks war is not worth the candle'.

9 January 1951
The first film ever to receive an 'X' certificate from the British Board of Censors opened in London. Called *Life Begins Tomorrow* it's been pretty much forgotten since.

10 January 1994
Clearly unable to wait, boxers Michael Bentt and Herbie Hide started fighting each other at the press conference in a London hotel where the announcement was made that they would have an official fight two months later.

11 January 1569
Britain got its first state lottery. In those days the prizes were rather smaller than today and punters bought their tickets at the door to St Paul's Cathedral.

14 January 1929
Two Harley Street surgeons cut their own throats after donating all their instruments to a local hospital.

17 January 1997
London radio stations banned all records by the group East 17 after band member Brian Harvey claimed ecstasy was a safe drug which made users feel great.

18 January 1936
Rudyard Kipling died in London aged seventy. Said to be the most popular and highest paid writer in the world, his death was promptly eclipsed by that of George V two days later.

19 January 1941
Prime Minister Winston Churchill unhesitatingly dismissed a snotty army officer who wrote to *The Times* insisting that even the bravest working- and lower-middle-class soldiers were not fit to be officers.

23 January 1985
The proceedings of the House of Lords were televised for the first time, but not many people tuned in to watch.

25 January 1905
The largest diamond ever found was dug up in a mine in South Africa. Brought to London it was presented to Edward VII, then cut into 105 gems and set into the Crown Jewels.

28 January 1939
The Thames burst its banks turning Eton College into an island. Unfazed by the drama, the boys cheerfully fed the swans from the windows of their school rooms.

29 January 1942
Desert Island Discs was first broadcast, presenter Roy Plomley going on to host a staggering 1,791 editions of the radio show.

2 February 1971
Buckingham Palace received an offer from Idi Amin – his country's self-proclaimed 'Ruler for Ever and Ever' – to marry Princess Anne in order to cement good relations between Uganda and the UK.

5 February 1924
The BBC's celebrated 'pips' from the Greenwich Observatory were broadcast for the first time ever.

7 February 1991
John Major and his Cabinet narrowly escaped injury after the IRA launched a mortar attack on Downing Street, firing three shells from a van parked nearby.

10 February 1840
Teen sweethearts Queen Victoria and Prince Albert of Saxe-Coburg-Gotha were married in St James's Palace, London at the tender age of just twenty.

16 February 1922
'Concrete Bob' McAlpine signed a contract to build the new Wembley Stadium at a price of £75,000. Ready for the following year's FA Cup Final it was completed within 300 days.

21 February 1938
American scientist W.H. Corrothors invented a miracle fabric called Nylon. He got the name by combining New York and London.

7 March 1975
While thumbing a ride home, hapless thief Sam Thomas mistakenly accepted a lift from a group of policemen, one of whom he had just burgled.

25 March 1947
Reg Dwight was born in a council house at 55 Pinner Hill Road, later adopting the name Elton John.

27 March 1996
The World Cup, which had been stolen just days earlier, was discovered in a London garden where it had been dug up by a dog called Pickles.

28 March 1912
The annual University Boat Race turned out to be something of a damp squib when both teams sank.

1 April 1968
One of the great London landowners, the Duke of Bedford was fined £50 for 'undertaking' on the M1. Police had recognised his numberplate, DOB1.

6 April 1965
The Kray twins were acquitted of demanding money with menaces, Eastender Ronnie telling the press outside the Old Bailey, 'definitely it's the quiet life for us from now on'.

7 April 1968
King Freddie of Buganda, who had earlier been seen around town with Princess Margaret and the Queen Mother, was found living on the dole in south London with friends slipping him the odd fiver every now and then.

9 April 1970
John, Paul, George and Ringo went their own separate ways after Paul petitioned the High Court to have the Beatles formally wound up.

10 April 1633
The first banana ever seen in Britain went on sale in London.

14 April 1967
Casino Royale premiered in London, an 'unofficial' Bond spoof featuring several different 007s played by David Niven, Woody Allen and Peter Sellers.

16 April 1969
HRH Princess Anne went to see the hippy musical *Hair* at the Shaftesbury Theatre. That she did caused some surprise as the performance included a scandalous nude sequence set to music.

23 April 1702
Queen Anne became the first British monarch to be carried to her coronation. Gout-ridden, she felt lousy despite having forked out an impressive £12 for a new wig.

1 May 1851
Queen Victoria opened the Great Exhibition held in the Crystal Palace in London's Hyde Park.

2 May 1536
Mary Queen of Scots was sent to the Tower.

3 May 1951
The Festival of Britain, a sort of spiritual forerunner of our own Millennium Dome but successful, opened on London's South Bank.

5 May 1980
Many millions of TV viewers watched as black-clad soldiers of the SAS successfully stormed the terrorist-held Iranian Embassy in London.

9 May 1949
The country's first automated launderette opened at 184 Queensway in Bayswater, West London.

11 May 1812
Spencer Perceval became the first British Prime Minister to be assassinated, cut down in the lobby of the House by an aggrieved Liverpudlian.

16 May 1983
Londoners experienced the inconvenience of wheel-clamps for the first time.

18 May 1955
The country's first Wimpy Bar opened in London. At the time it was heralded as the birth of fast food in Britain, everyone having conveniently forgotten about fish and chips.

23 May 1701
The notorious Scottish pirate Captain Kidd was executed at Wapping, despite having earlier been promised a royal pardon if he and his crew of cut-throats gave themselves up.

25 May 1967
John Lennon wheeled out his new Phantom limousine with a swirly rainbow psychedelic paint job. It cost an extra £1,000, a Rolls-Royce spokesman sniffily describing its appearance as 'unfortunate'.

1 June 836
Viking raiders succeeded in sailing up the Thames to pillage London. The same day in 1915 Londoners were to take another pounding, in the first ever Zeppelin raid on the capital.

3 June 1931
The BBC transmitted its first ever outside broadcast, a single van-mounted camera being used to beam back pictures of the Derby live from Epsom.

5 June 1939
An assassin attempted to shoot the Duchess of Kent in London, but she didn't realise what was happening and went off to see *Wuthering Heights* at the cinema.

14 June 1380
Revolting peasants occupied London and cut off the head of Archbishop Simon of Sudbury. His skull can still be seen today on display in the Suffolk market town from which he took his name.

17 June 1959
Rhinestoned pianist Liberace won £8,000 in damages from the *Daily Mirror* after a London court rejected the newspaper's allegation that he might be gay.

19 June 1944
One of Hitler's new flying bombs – the V1 or Doodlebug – landed on the Wellington Barracks next door to Buckingham Palace, killing Lord Edward Hay and several friends of the royal family.

21 June 1997
England's cricketers were all out for just 77 runs, their lowest total at Lords since 1888. One Aussie bowler took 8 wickets for a measly 38 runs.

22 June 1993
A spectator at Wimbledon was banned from the courtside seats after shouting rude things at Steffi Graf.

23 June 1951
Two missing 'diplomats' called Guy Burgess and Donald Maclean were presumed to have fled to Moscow after lunching at the Royal Automobile Club in Pall Mall.

27 June 1923
The Times carried an advertisement headed 'Seeing by Wireless'. After years of trying, John Logie Baird had finally invented the television.

30 June 1967
A sky-blue Bentley collected Mick Jagger from Wormwood Scrubs and Keith Richards from Brixton respectively, where they had been sent for drugs offences.

2 July 1995
American tennis player Jeff Turango was fined £10,000 by the Wimbledon authorities after his wife slapped an umpire.

4 July 1829
Britain's first scheduled omnibus service started, running regularly from Marylebone Road to the Bank of England.

11 July 1969
Elizabeth Taylor hit the headlines after turning up at the annual Eton versus Harrow cricket match wearing a yellow kaftan and her famously huge diamond ring.

13 July 1955
Britain hanged a female murderer for the last time when 28-year-old Ruth Ellis went to the gallows for shooting her lover.

20 July 1535
Margaret Roper recovered the head of her father from a pole on London Bridge. Thomas More had been beheaded by Henry VIII after his refusal to accept the king's marriage to Anne Boleyn.

28 July 1964
Sir Winston Churchill awoke to find himself no longer a Member of Parliament for the first time since February 1901.

2 August 1957
Lord Altrincham repeated rude comments about the Queen on the wireless and was afterwards punched on the nose by a listener who was later fined £1.

4 August 2000
Queen Elizabeth the Queen Mother became the first royal to reach 100, thereby qualifying for a 'telemessage' from her daughter.

10 August 1925
The Maharajah of Patiala took over an entire floor of the Savoy. Not content with occupying 35 luxury suites, according to the press he also wore special underpants costing more than £200 a pair.

15 August 1950
Play stopped briefly at the Oval for an announcement that Princess Anne had been born.

25 August 1969
The Shell Oil heiress Olga Deterding, who had moved back into the Ritz despite having announced earlier that she was giving up the high life to help lepers, split up with TV presenter Alan Whicker.

31 August 1888
The mutilated body of Jack the Ripper's first victim was discovered. Mary Ann Nichols – known as Polly – was found in Buck's Row in London's East End.

4 September 1752
Nothing at all happened because 3–13 September had been cancelled that year so the official calendar could be changed to a more accurate system.

5 September 1988
No Sex Please We're British, the West End's longest-running comedy, closed after sixteen years and an incredible 6,671 performances.

10 September 1897
After crashing into a shop front in Bond Street, London cabbie George Smith became the first person in the country to be convicted of drunk-driving. He was fined £1.

11 September 1978
Georgi Markov, a Bulgarian defector working for the BBC, was stabbed and killed in the street using a brolly fitted with a poisoned tip.

19 September 1960
While a new dance craze rocked America and Chubby Checker's 'Twist' rocketed up the charts, traffic wardens hit swinging London for the first time and issued 344 parking tickets on their first day.

21 September 1915
A man called Mr C.H. Chubb paid £6,600 at auction for a collection of old rocks. Three years later he donated his purchase, Stonehenge, to the nation.

26 September 1963
Lord Denning's official report into the Profumo Affair went on sale in London and became the year's surprise best-seller with more than 100,000 copies selling in the first 24 hours.

2 October 1909
History was made in south-west London when Harlequins played Richmond in the first rugby match ever to be played on Twickers' hallowed turf.

8 October 1965
Britain got a new tallest building when the Post Office Tower topped out at 580ft (plus another 70ft for the radio mast).

13 October 1884
Greenwich was officially adopted as the universal meridian of longitude, since when standard times around the world have been measured from this point.

15 October 1066
Rumours began circulating in London that King Harold had only been wounded. Not true of course, otherwise it really would have been one in the eye for the Normans.

26 October 1958
BOAC started its first scheduled jet airliner service from London to New York. (Coincidentally on the same day in 1929 Mrs T.W. Evans had become the first woman ever to give birth on board an aircraft.)

29 October 1618
Sir Walter Raleigh was executed. In an early attempt at a soundbite, he told the crowd at the foot of the scaffold, 'this is sharp medicine, but it is a physician for all diseases'.

1 November 1959
The M1 opened linking London with the north. There was no official speed restriction until 1963 when a temporary 70mph limit was made permanent after an AC Cobra sports car was clocked at 196mph.

2 November 1848
W.H. Smith opened the first ever railway station bookstall in Little Grosvenor Street, London. The company was actually founded by a woman, Anna Smith, but is named after her son to whom she bequeathed the business.

3 November 1960
Cleared in the High Court of publishing obscene material after a lengthy and notorious trial, Penguin Books announced it was printing an extra 250,000 copies of *Lady Chatterley's Lover* to cope with the demand.

6 November 1975
The Sex Pistols punk rock group gave their first public concert at a London art school but after less than 10 minutes were told to pack up and go home.

12 November 1974
Somebody caught a salmon in the River Thames, the first time such a thing had happened since the 1840s.

18 November 1836
W.S. Gilbert of Gilbert & Sullivan fame was born in London. The S, incidentally, stands for Schwenck.

19 November 1987
At the Royal Albert Hall a new world record was achieved when an enormously rare 1931 Bugatti Royale motor car was sold at auction for a staggering £5.5million.

25 November 1952
Agatha Christie's classic whodunnit *The Mousetrap* opened in the West End. Still showing today, it has become the longest-running stage play of all time.

26 November 1964
Mick Jagger was fined a tenner for driving without insurance, his lawyer telling the court the Rolling Stones were not 'long-haired idiots, but highly intelligent university men'.

7 December 1817
Captain Bligh of the *Bounty* (and of Lambeth), apparently a good sailor but a harsh disciplinarian, was put into an open boat and cast adrift by a band of mutineers.

11 December 1987
At a film memorabilia sale at Christie's, Charlie Chaplin's famous trademark cane and bowler hat were auctioned for an incredible £82,500.

25 December 1254
King Henry III sat down to a Christmas dinner comprising no fewer than 100 wild boar.

30 December 1919
The first woman law student was admitted to study at Lincoln's Inn in London.

31 December 1923
The chimes of Big Ben were first broadcast by the BBC – and they still are, live at 6 o'clock every evening, via a microphone hidden behind the famous clock.